9 Plays
for the Christian in All of Us

DARRON BAILEY JR.

WESTBOW
PRESS®
A DIVISION OF THOMAS NELSON
& ZONDERVAN

WestBow Press books may be ordered through booksellers or by contacting:

WestBow Press
A Division of Thomas Nelson & Zondervan
1663 Liberty Drive
Bloomington, IN 47403
www.westbowpress.com
1 (866) 928-1240

Scripture taken from the King James Version of the Bible.

ISBN: 978-1-5127-7671-3 (sc)
ISBN: 978-1-5127-7673-7 (hc)
ISBN: 978-1-5127-7672-0 (e)

Library of Congress Control Number: 2017902815

Print information available on the last page.

WestBow Press rev. date: 03/14/2017

Dedications

I dedicate this, my second book to ever be published, to my Dad, **Reverend Darron Bailey Sr.** You are the best father I could have ever asked for. There is no substitution. You encouraged me to pursue my dreams and helped me realize exactly what they were. Your attention to detail helped me understand how to better myself in school, in music, in writing, even in preaching. The prayers and guidance you gave to me growing up have been engraved into my mind and my heart. You certainly bring new meaning to Proverbs 22:6 "Train up a child in the way he should go: and when he is old, he will not depart from it." I could never mention any of my talents, without first mentioning how you got me into them.

When I'd be up late hours of the night writing this book, you'd always check up on me to see if everything was going well. You're never afraid to give me your honest opinion on my work, and that goes a long way, especially from parent to child. You are not the type of person who'd lie to me about my work, and that is why I feel such a great level of achievement when I hear you say you enjoy the ones you do. You are, and always have been, a fair father and a best friend to me. When I had no one to talk to, I had you. When I had no one to play with, I had you. When I had no one to defend me, I had you. My prayer to God is that you will have life and that you might have it more abundantly. I pray that you will live long on this earth and be happy with all the decisions you make. Because every decision you have ever made for me, I have no regrets, because they all shaped me into who I am today. I love you Dad.

I also dedicate this book to my mother, **Reverend Doctor Sanneth Brown.** You are the greatest mother I could have ever asked for. You are one in a million and that is not an exaggeration. When I think of someone with the purist of heart, you are the first person I think of. You'd read me bed time stories when I was a toddler and as I grew older, these stories became Bible stories. Truly you have trained me in the ways of the gospel and I can't thank you enough. You are always lending your ear to hear my stories, you are always lending advice to make my showmanship better, you are always lending your wisdom to keep me out of harms way. Your love for me is beyond description. You have always discerned, decreed and declared over all my life's endeavours. You not only demonstrated true agape parental love to me, but you believed that all my dreams, visions, and revelations would be accomplished. Your daily prayer of authority and Holy Spirit filled decrees over my life, will always be remembered. The publishing of this book is also one of your prophetic prophesies coming to pass. The Holy Spirit prophetic anointed ministry within you is great and mighty because of the purpose God has given you. I am a million times thankful for being blessed as your son.

I will never forget your recital of Matthew 10:16 "Behold, I send you forth as sheep in the midst of wolves: be ye therefore wise as serpents, and harmless as doves." Not a day goes by without me remembering this. I thank you for all the prayers and fasting that you've done for this books success. I will never forget all the prayers and fasting that you did for my life and even the ones we've done together. I am truly blessed by God to be able to say that you are my mother. My prayer for you is that you shall not die, but live, and declare the works of The Lord. You are a mighty force to be reckoned with and I love you Mom.

I'd like to dedicate this book to my grandmother, **Beryl Abdulie-Gibson**, or as I like to call her, Mommies. I love you so very much and will never forget all that you have done in my life. You always ask me how I am doing when ever we meet. You are never afraid to say you love me and you are always so generous to me. For as long as I can remember, you've always encouraged me to be happy with the love that the Lord shows me every day I wake up. You always said that that was enough reason to praise Jehovah. Nothing you've ever said to me lacked meaning, and every moment I share with you, fills my heart with love, laughter, and life. I love you, Mommies.

I'd like to dedicate this book to my late grandfather, Late **Bishop Prophet Elijah Brown**. I thank him for the mantle he passed down to my mother, that will one day be passed down to me. The ministry he left behind has surrounded me all of my life. The blessing on my life is all thanks to him, so I decided to dedicate this to him. None of my work could be possible without his influence over my life.

Next, I'd like to dedicate this book to my late grandmother, Late **Evangelist Estella Euphemia Brown**. She was such a loving grandmother. She always hugged me and would tell me how much I meant to her. She would always greet me with a smile and would tell me that I am blessed by the Lord before I left her house. She was such a peaceful person to me. I thank her for all of the encouragements and love she gave me.

Finally, I'd like to dedicate this book to my late grandfather, Late **Hosley Bailey**. Had it not been for him, I wouldn't be alive today.

Acknowledgements

Latoya Brown. I remember all of the times you babysat me. You've been in my life for as long as I can remember. I also remember every time you encouraged me to pursue my dreams. You always speak victory in my life and I am thankful for every moment we spend together. I love you, cousin Latoya.

Patricia Bryan. You are such an enthusiastic and helpful cousin. You always lend a hand to help me how ever you can and I appreciate it. Thank you for your fasting and praying for success in these. You even went as far as to encourage me to get these plays published specifically. Thank you for believing they are worth more than just a simple church play.

Mildred Ellis. I remember when we first met. You were full of joy, kindness, and honesty. I am happy to see that none of that has changed. Your radiant smile and joyous laughter always makes my day a lot better. From one writer to another, I look forward to your books and plays in the future.

Chelsey Clarke. Thank you for all of your encouragements when it came to writing these plays. It meant a lot being able to speak to you about acting and certain roles in these plays. You obviously showed interest in this and I hope you pursue writing as well.

Faurel Davis. My Precious godmother. Thank you for praying and fasting for my success and achievements. You've been a great support to my mother and I. Thank you for not forgetting me, and loving me for who I am, and treating me like family.

Mike Bailey. Thank you for being a great uncle. Thank you for encouraging me to follow in my mother's foot steps and to always stay close to her. I will never forget those words. They fill me with gladness and give me words to stay true to. Thank you very much.

Late aunt in law, Ava. I will never forget the words she told me before passing. She said the day she met me as a baby, she saw a glean in my eye. She told me I was destined for greatness and that I must never forget who my mother is. I thank her for every encouragement she gave me. I will never ever forget her.

Tajmic Bailey. My brotherly cousin. I remember when we were really young and you told me never to give up on what ever I put my mind to. I vividly remember all the days you'd tell me never to be afraid of the things and people around me. Your words still resonate with me to this day. Thank you very much for everything you shared with me as a child. They still impact me today.

Minetha Brown. Thank you for being such a great aunt. You've always been an encouraging and uplifting person in my life. Thank you for all your words, prayers, and fasting. It means a lot to me.

Carmetta Clarke. Thank you for always trusting my judgement. Thank you for never doubting my capabilities and thank you for encouraging me to do new things with my writing. You are a great support and you always help with transportation for actors and actresses. Thank you very much.

Reverend Vernal Brown. Thank you for always believing in me. Thank you for always encouraging me not to pay attention to discouragers around. You always tell me to keep my spirits high and I always will.

Rudroy Brown. Thank you so much for always telling me how much I mean to you. Thank you for always encouraging me to follow and help my mother in every way I can.

Everton Wheatle. Thank you for encouraging me to get back into writing after high school. I give God thanks every time I write a play and I never forget that you encouraged me to get back to it.

Phillippa Stewart. May the Lord bless you with happiness and joy. You always know how to make me smile and I appreciate every word of encouragement you have given me in the past, and I will hold them closely to me in the future.

Veronica Morgan. Thank you very much for never losing faith in me. You are so special and kind to me. Thank you for all your love and all your support. Never lose your humor.

Pauline Fuller. Thank you very much for your never-failing loyalty. You are an inspiration to many and your love is endless. Continue to do the work of God.

Shermane Watkin. You always tell me I am talented and you always look forward to when I write a play. Thank you very much for having faith in me.

Minister Karen Brown. Your presence is always a joy. Thank you for trusting in my writing abilities and helping as an actress when it is needed.

Carolyn Smart. You always acknowledge God first in all that you do, and encourage me to do the same. Thank you for everything.

Minister Karen Grant. Thank you for your acting, fasting, prayer, and encouragements over my life. Your scripture choices are well received.

Theresa Wright. You are special and always encourage me to pursue my writing. Thank you for your support and acting.

Minister Brian Robinson. Peace unto you. You are a very meek person and always speak to me as an equal and not just a young man. Thank you for your support and thanks for all your acting ability.

Jeffery Jennings. You truly are a helpful person and thank you for your acting abilities. You will not be forgotten and I am grateful for you.

Kriston Brown. You, my cousin, have been in my life for as long as I can remember. You have really grown and are always an encouraging person to me. May your talent shine even brighter in the future.

Treyvon Brown. You are special and you are not made to be a follower. Your acting and dancing is a special tool to make your mark on this world. You are talented and will never be forgotten by me. Thank you for everything you've done in my life. Keep the faith and stay at peace with the Lord. You once told me that you trust anything I write, I will never forget that and I pray that I never disappoint.

Terrence Brown. I will never forget all the times we spent together coming up with stories with our action figures. I'm glad I can write Bible related stories now. Thank you for always being someone I can depend on. Never lose your focus and remember you are a child of God.

Elliott Lewis. You are a talented writer. Never forget that. Pursue your writing career and God will use you tremendously. But never forget to show love in all your work. You really bring new experiences into my life every time we work together. Thank you for everything.

John Haye. You are always enthusiastic about acting and I appreciate every time we ever do a show. Thank you for your enthusiasm and your optimism. Never lose that.

Ishmael Brown. God is ready to do a new thing in your life. You are so skilled and so talented; I can't wait to see the work you do in the future. Thank you for all of your acting.

Tiana Brown. Stay close to your family and remember they will always be your family. You are talented and educated and have a lot to offer the world. Thank you for every time we've ever worked together.

Pastor Anthony Bartley. You are quick-witted, thoughtful, and insightful. Thank you for always encouraging my writing and approaching acting with great enthusiasm.

Murine Blake. What a wonder it is to have you in my life as a godmother. You are such a fabulous and kind hearted person. Your generosity is easily seen and greatly appreciated. I thank you for everything you've done for me and for my family.

Yvonne Bell. To a fellow Christ group member, you are such a helpful, generous, and loyal person. You've helped and prayed for me in so many situations. Your smile is one of richness and tranquility. Your laugh is contagious and always needed whenever I hear it. Thank you for the help you've given both me and my family. Your generosity will never be forgotten.

Who Am I?

CHARACTERS	ACTORS
The Man in White (Understanding)	
Soccer Player/Moses (Leadership)	
Lawyer/Jeremiah (Confidence)	
Boxer/Samson (Strength)	
Poet/David (Passion)	
Soldier/Peter (Determination)	
Outcast/Solomon (Wisdom)	

Guideline

* All character names are centred and in capitals.
* All dialogue is placed under the respective character's name.
* Anything in (brackets) is an action.
* A costume reflecting each respective character is required

Side Notes

The words next to the names are personality traits. They'll give you an idea on how to act them out. Highlight your parts! Try to remember the line before yours so you know your cue.

Setting

The front of the sanctuary will be where all scenes take place.

ALL (EXCEPT THE MAN IN WHITE)
(Enters the sanctuary frantically, complaining while in character. Walks to the front of the sanctuary.)

THE MAN IN WHITE
(Enters sanctuary.)
My brothers!

ALL (EXCEPT THE MAN IN WHITE)
(Freezes in spot.)

THE MAN IN WHITE
(Walks to the front of the sanctuary.)
God created man in his own image. Show yourselves in all respects to be a model of good works, and in your teaching, show leadership, confidence, strength, passion, determination, wisdom, and understanding of who you are. So allow me to ask ...
(Walks over to SOCCER PLAYER.)
Who are you?

SOCCER PLAYER
(Unfreezes.)
Who am I? Well, as you can see by my medals, I am the star player and captain of my soccer team! No matter what comes my way, I know that with enough practice and dedication, I can succeed.

THE MAN IN WHITE
And what about your team?

SOCCER PLAYER
What team?
(Sighs.)
They're so stubborn. If I say, "Guard left," some of them guard right. If I say, "Wait," a few will get impatient and go. Yet they always look to me for answers, and half the time, I don't even think they listen to anything I say.

THE MAN IN WHITE

Leadership isn't an easy trait to carry. Just as the body is one and has many members, all the members of the body, though many, are one body.

SOCCER PLAYER

I'm sorry. What was that?

THE MAN IN WHITE

A parable. What I'm trying to say is just because there are many people on your team who don't cooperate, that doesn't mean that they're not a part of the team. Why not try going over your play before each game and asking whether or not everyone understands? If they don't, then break it down so they do.

SOCCER PLAYER

Wow, that sounds like a great idea! That way I'll know who needs help and how to help them. Thanks a lot.

(Slowly exits sanctuary.)

THE MAN IN WHITE

Be patient, Moses, and you will be remembered as a man of great leadership! Well, now I know who that was. But I must ask ...

(Walks over to LAWYER.)

Who are you?

LAWYER

(Panics.)

Me? I'm late, is what I am! I need to hurry up and get to the courtroom before the trial begins, or I might lose my job. But what if they don't understand what I'm saying? What if I don't deliver properly and mess up?

(Weeps.)

I just can't do it! I'm way too young, anyway! What was I thinking becoming a lawyer at this age? I'm in way over my head.

(Falls to knees.)

THE MAN IN WHITE

Hey, hey. Weep not, Jeremiah, for God is with you.

LAWYER

Huh? What did you say?

THE MAN IN WHITE

Let no one despise you for your youth, but set the believers an example in speech, in conduct, in love, in faith, and in purity.

LAWYER

I don't understand.

THE MAN IN WHITE

All it takes to win this case is speech, conduct, and faith. You only need three of those five to win, so there's nothing to be afraid of.

LAWYER

You're right!
    (Counts off fingers while slowly exiting sanctuary.)
Speech, conduct, faith! Speech, conduct, faith! Speech, conduct, faith! This is easy!
    (Exits.)

THE MAN IN WHITE

Weep no more, Jeremiah. You will be remembered as a man of great confidence despite all the odds against you. It was nice getting to know him, but now I must know …
    (Walks over to BOXER.)
Who are you?

BOXER

Who am I?
(Flexes.)
I'm the guy that nightmares are afraid of. I've defeated at least 9,999 guys in the ring and still haven't broken a sweat. Tomorrow's the big match against the heavyweight champion. I hear he's as strong as a lion.

THE MAN IN WHITE

Ah, I thought I recognized you, Samson. Surely you plan on training for such an occasion, right?

BOXER

Pssh. Yeah, right!
(Puts arm on THE MAN IN WHITE's shoulder.)
Who needs to train? When you're as strong as me, all you need to think about is drinking and being merry.

THE MAN IN WHITE

(Takes arm off of shoulder.)
But what about your oath to your coach? You're not supposed to be drinking before a match, or even at all. And what about your oath to God? Do not get drunk with wine, for that is debauchery, but be filled with the Spirit. Wine is a mocker, strong drink a brawler, and whoever is led astray by it is not wise.

BOXER

What are you? Some kind of undercover trainer?

THE MAN IN WHITE

You could say that.

BOXER

Well, fine. I guess what you're saying is right. Guess I'd better start training.
(Slowly exits sanctuary.)

THE MAN IN WHITE

Be cautious, Samson, and in due time, you will be remembered as a man of great strength … Oh.
(Places hands over mouth to shout.)
And don't let anyone cut your hair off! What a character he was.
(Walks over to POET.)
I think it's about time I learn what kind of character you are.

POET

(Walks away slowly while looking at paper with pen in hand.)
Yeah, yeah, hang on. Do you know what rhymes with way?

THE MAN IN WHITE

Day, ray, play, say, hey, Jay, Kay …

POET

Oh, oh, okay. I got it. *Gweh.*
(Writes it down on paper.)
I'm a genius!

THE MAN IN WHITE

Say, whatcha writin' there? Dav—

POET

Oh, hey! You. Give me a beat.

THE MAN IN WHITE

Well, okay then.
(Beat boxes.)

POET

(Raps.)
Hangin' with my Jesus, day and night.
Prayin' that my brothers won't start a fight.
The giants keep standin' in my way.
I keep my cool and just tell 'em, "*Gweh!*"

Roses are red, violets are purple …
Ah, man. Nothing rhymes with purple!

THE MAN IN WHITE

(Stops beat boxing.)
That was actually pretty decent.

POET

You think? 'Cause no one else thinks so. They all say my work is no good
and I'm completely talentless.

THE MAN IN WHITE

Do you believe them?

POET

(Shakes head and smiles.)
Nope!
(Slowly exits sanctuary.)

THE MAN IN WHITE

(Laughs.)
Be ye steadfast and unmovable, David, and you will be remembered as a
man of great passion in all that you—Wait, wait! Door hinge! Door hinge
rhymes with orange! That was fun.
(Walks over to SOLDIER.)
Now …

SOLDIER

(Opens map.)
The enemy's coming in from around the northern areas. Thankfully, HQ's
in the south end. I've got a fleet protecting both the east and west rivers,
which means—

THE MAN IN WHITE

Who are—

SOLDIER

We're smack-dab in the middle of enemy territory. But that's okay. We'll have better terrain and a bagload of options.

THE MAN IN WHITE

I beg your par—

SOLDIER

Now, this might be risky, but if we use the phalanx formation, I think we can avoid a lot of unwanted kinetic activity. After that, everything should be five by five and ready to go.
(Pats THE MAN IN WHITE's back.)

THE MAN IN WHITE

(Smiles.)
Bold, committed, and quick to answer. You must be Peter. Say, let me ask you something. Have you tried praying before battle?

SOLDIER

What do you mean?

THE MAN IN WHITE

Well, you obviously seem confident in the situation at hand, but that doesn't mean you shouldn't pray before battle. Don't forget that pride goes before destruction, and a haughty spirit before stumbling.

SOLDIER

Believe me when I say that I am a faithful man. I pray whenever I can, and I read the Bible in my free time.

THE MAN IN WHITE

Okay. Just remember, Peter, that even though all may fall away because of you, I will never fall away.

SOLDIER

Hmm.

(Slowly exits sanctuary.)

That sounds familiar. I wonder who said that?

THE MAN IN WHITE

(Smiles.)

Someone very close to me. One step at a time, Peter, and you'll be remembered as a man of great determination.

(Walks over to OUTCAST.)

Now, it all comes down to you. So may I ask, Who are you?

OUTCAST

(Sitting.)

I'm a nobody. My life is a lie. My parents are divorced, my mother could barely support me, I've given into the temptations of alcohol, and I've hit rock bottom. No one cares about me. I watch people pass by day in and day out, but there's no one watching me.

THE MAN IN WHITE

Are you done with the self-pitying? Have you finished all your brooding and loathing? Do you think you're ready to make the difference in your life?

OUTCAST

See? No one understands! My life is a living tragedy!

THE MAN IN WHITE

So what? I never said the road would be easy. Fact is, being a man is hard. But are you going to let that prevent you from following your calling?

OUTCAST

My calling?

THE MAN IN WHITE

God has given you enough knowledge and personal experience to teach others about the troubles of giving in to temptation! You can help others who are going through relationship problems, and in doing so, you can find a way to help both them and yourself. After all, God said he will not suffer you to be tempted beyond what you are able to bear.

(Helps OUTCAST stand up.)

Be strong, Solomon, and you will be remembered as a man of great wisdom.

OUTCAST

Wait a minute. Who are you?

THE MAN IN WHITE

Who am I? Well, where do I begin? Alpha or Omega? Beginning or end?

OUTCAST

No way! You're—

THE MAN IN WHITE

My brothers!

ALL

(Re-enter the sanctuary one by one.)

THE MAN IN WHITE

God created man in his own image. Show yourselves in all respects to be a model of good works, and in your teaching, show—

SOCCER PLAYER

Leadership.

LAWYER

Confidence.

BOXER

Strength.

POET

Passion.

SOLDIER

Determination.

OUTCAST

Wisdom.

THE MAN IN WHITE

And understanding of who you are. *Who are we?*

ALL

We are men. Mighty men of valour. Today, we are here to declare victory.

THE END

Army of God

CHARACTERS	ACTORS
The General	
Peter (Impulsive/Courageous)	
James, son of Zebedee (Vengeful/Loyal)	
John (Judgmental/Bold)	
Andrew (Curious/Enthusiastic)	
Philip (Literal/Helpful)	
Bartholomew (Skeptical/Honest)	
Matthew (Apologetic/Sociable)	
Thomas (Doubtful/Faithful)	
Young James, son of Alphaeus (Silent/Listener)	
Thaddaeus, aka Jude (Confused/Inquisitive)	
Simon the Zealot (Patriotic/Sacrificial)	
Judas Iscariot (Deceitful/Remorseful)	

Guideline

* All character names are centred and in capitals.
* All dialogue is placed under the respective character's name.
* Anything in (brackets) is an action.
* A costume reflecting each respective character is required.

Side Notes

The words next to the names are personality traits. They'll give you an idea on how to act them out. Highlight your parts! Try to remember the line before yours so you know your cue. In your free time, practice push-ups! You'll be doing them in this play.

Setting

The front of the sanctuary will be where all scenes take place. It is both the lounge and the training field. Philip, Bartholomew, Thomas, Thaddaeus, and Simon are playing an active game together. Matthew, Young James, and Judas are counting money on a table. Peter, James, John, Andrew, and the General aren't on stage yet. All are wearing army gear and colours. Blue jumpsuits are worn by the fishermen (Peter, James, John, and Andrew) for the whole scene. There are chairs in the lounge.

BARTHOLOMEW
(While playing the game, knocks table over.)

JUDAS
What do you think you're doing?

SIMON
We're trying to play a game here!

JUDAS
And we're trying to do business here. Do you mind taking it somewhere else?

BARTHOLOMEW
Last time I checked, this was our lounge.

JUDAS
(Stands up)
And last time I checked, you were a grown man. It's strange how the eyes can deceive you.

BARTHOLOMEW
(Walks over to Judas.)
What are you trying to say?

SIMON & PHILIP
(Rush to hold Bartholomew back.)

MATTHEW
(Steps in front of Judas.)
Forgive my friend. He's been having a bad day.

THOMAS
(Arms crossed)
Seems like he's always having a bad day.

JUDAS
(Tries to go through Matthew.)
Excuse me?

THADDAEUS
(Rushes over.)
Whoa, whoa. What's going on over here?

YOUNG JAMES
(Stands up to speak.)

MATTHEW
Nothing! Nothing! My friend would like to …
(Looks at Judas)
Apologize! For his crass behaviour.

YOUNG JAMES
(Sits back down)

JUDAS
(Whispers)
I'm sorry.

BARTHOLOMEW
(Cuffs ear)
What was that? Couldn't hear you over that attitude of yours.

JUDAS
I said I'm sorry!
(Sits back down)

SIMON
All right, then.
(Begins to walk away with the rest of the boys)

THOMAS

(Coughs)
Tax collectors.

MATTHEW & YOUNG JAMES

(Stand up)
Hey, hey, hey.
(Walk over to them)

JUDAS

(Stays seated and begins to steal money from the table)

PETER, JAMES, JOHN & ANDREW
(Enter stage with big bag of fish over their shoulders)

PETER

All right, ladies, simmer down, simmer down.

THADDAEUS

Did you guys bring some fish for us?

JOHN

(Sarcastically)
No, we're just carrying these bags 'cause they make us look pretty.

PHILIP

You know, it does really bring out your eyes.

ALL (except Philip)

(Stare at Philip)

PHILIP

But it does …

JAMES

(Puts bag down and pats Philip's head)

Sit down.

ALL

(Take a seat)

PETER

All right, listen up, 'cause we're only going to do this once. Philip!

PHILIP

I'm Philip!

PETER

(Gives fish to Philip)

Bartholomew!

BARTHOLOMEW

Greetings.

PETER

(Gives fish to Bartholomew)

James!

YOUNG JAMES

(Stands up to speak)

PETER

Son of Zebedee!

YOUNG JAMES

(Sits back down)

JAMES

Over here.
(Takes fish)
All right, my turn. Matthew!

MATTHEW

Huh? Oh, sorry—that's me.

JAMES

(Gives fish to Matthew)
Thomas!

THOMAS

Are you sure this fish is fresh?

JAMES

(Gives fish to Thomas)
John!

JOHN

Yup!
(Takes fish)
Here we go now. James!

YOUNG JAMES

(Looks around, then to John)

JOHN

Son of Alphaeus!

YOUNG JAMES

(Rushes to take fish from John, then returns to his seat)

JOHN

Thaddaeus!

THADDAEUS

Wait. Why are we all getting fish?

JOHN

(Gives fish to Thaddaeus)
Andrew!

ANDREW

(Takes fish)
For me? You shouldn't have. Simon!

PETER

Cool name.

JUDAS

(Begins to sneak away with all the money he's been stealing)

SIMON

Thanks.
(Takes fish from Andrew)

ANDREW

Peter!

PETER

Mine.
(Takes fish from Andrew)

ANDREW

And that leaves ... Judas!

JUDAS

(Loudly drops bags of money by accident)
Uh, yes?

ALL (EXCEPT JUDAS)

(Stare at Judas)

MATTHEW

Hey, is that our money?

JUDAS

N-no. I won this ... in the lottery.

THOMAS

(Crosses arms)
For some reason, I doubt that.

JUDAS

Fine, fine. You caught me. Give me my fish.
(Takes fish from Andrew and sits down)

PETER

All right, let us bow our heads and say grace.

ALL

(Put hands together, bow their heads)
Amen!
(Begin to eat)

THE GENERAL

(Enter stage)
Apostles! Attention!

ALL (EXCEPT THE GENERAL)

(Drop fish and stand at attention)

THE GENERAL

(Paces in front of them)

As you know, today is our final training day. This will determine which of you is strong, smart, and creative enough to be promoted to the next rank as my disciple. You'd better stay sharp and act accordingly, because there can only be one. Peter! James! John! Andrew!

PETER, JOHN, ANDREW & YOUNG JAMES

(Shocked)

Yes, sir?

THE GENERAL

What?

(Points to Young James)

No, not you, James!

(Points to James)

You, James!

JAMES

Yes, sir?

THE GENERAL

You four, step forward.

PETER, JAMES, JOHN & ANDREW

(Step forward)

THE GENERAL

Do you mind telling me why you four aren't wearing your uniforms? Do you not like the way it looks? Are you afraid of what people may think of you? Or perhaps a better question would be where you were earlier.

PETER

We were fishing!

JAMES

On a boat!

JOHN

With a net!

ANDREW

It's no joke.

THE GENERAL

Fishing, eh? A bit of a morning meal before training? How thoughtful of
you. Was there any for me?

ALL

(Look around at each silently)

THE GENERAL

Unwilling to make the sacrifice, I see. Ten push-ups, all of you!

ALL (EXCEPT THE GENERAL)

Ugh!
   (Begin push-ups. Judas cheats by not doing all ten)

THE GENERAL

   (Pacing while counting each number)
One, two, three, four, five, six, seven, eight, nine, ten! All rise!

ALL (EXCEPT THE GENERAL)

   (Stand up)

THE GENERAL

Attention!

ALL (EXCEPT THE GENERAL)

(Stand at attention)

THE GENERAL

At ease!

ALL (EXCEPT THE GENERAL)
(Stand at ease)

THE GENERAL
(Pacing)
All right, good hustle, everyone. But unfortunately, one of your brothers was holding back.
(Stops in front of Judas)
Don't think I didn't notice you, Judas.

JUDAS

I have no idea what you're talking about!

THE GENERAL

Proverbs 12:22? Anyone?

PHILIP

"Lying lips are abomination to the Lord: but they that deal truly are his delight."

THE GENERAL

Ten-four, Philip. And just for that, Judas, you can clean up all the fish around us.

JUDAS

As if I care.

THE GENERAL

Excuse me?

JUDAS

I said, "I'll be right there."
(Cleans up fish and moves seats aside)

THE GENERAL

Judas has given me a good idea. How about we play a little game? It'll get the stress of training off your mind before we begin. Psalms 1:1! Peter!

PETER

"Blessed *is* the man that walketh not in the counsel of the ungodly, nor standeth in the way of sinners, nor sitteth in the seat of the scornful."

THE GENERAL

Good. Now, 1 Timothy 6:11! James!

YOUNG JAMES

But as for—

THE GENERAL

Not you, James! The other James, the son of Zebedee! And can we stick to the King James Version, please?

JAMES

"But thou, O man of God, flee these things; and follow after righteousness, godliness, faith, love, patience, meekness."

THE GENERAL

Excellent. James 5:12! John!

JOHN

"But above all things, my brethren, swear not, neither by heaven, neither by the earth, neither by any other oath: but let your yea be yea; and *your* nay, nay; lest ye fall into condemnation."

THE GENERAL

Fantastic. Psalms 112:1. Andrew!

ANDREW

"Praise ye the LORD. Blessed is the man that feareth the LORD, that delighteth greatly in his commandments."

THE GENERAL

Extraordinary. Now, 1 Corinthians 16:13! Philip!

PHILIP

"Watch ye, stand fast in the faith, quit you like men, be strong."

THE GENERAL

Admirable. Psalms 37:23! Bartholomew!

BARTHOLOMEW

"The steps of a good man are ordered by the LORD: and he delighteth in his way."

THE GENERAL

Mesmerizing. Ephesians 6:4! Matthew!

MATTHEW

"And, ye fathers, provoke not your children to wrath: but bring them up in the nurture and admonition of the Lord."

THE GENERAL

Terrific. Colossians 3:19! Thomas!

THOMAS

"Husbands, love your wives, and be not bitter against them."

THE GENERAL

Superb. Genesis 1:26. James! Son of Alphaeus! Young James!

YOUNG JAMES

(Points at himself)

Me?

THE GENERAL

Do you see any other James's here?

YOUNG JAMES

"And God said, Let us make man in our image, after our likeness: and let them have dominion over the fish of the sea, and over the fowl of the air, and over the cattle, and over all the earth, and over every creeping thing that creepeth upon the earth."

THE GENERAL

Splendid. Proverbs 27:17! Thaddaeus!

THADDAEUS

"Iron sharpeneth iron; so a man sharpeneth the countenance of his friend."

THE GENERAL

Amazing. Let's flip that around. Proverbs 17:27! Simon!

SIMON

"He that hath knowledge spareth his words: and a man of understanding is of an excellent spirit."

THE GENERAL

Magnificent. Judges 6:12! Judas!

JUDAS

(Is sitting down, but rushes to his place before THE GENERAL notices)
"And the angel of the LORD appeared unto him, and said unto him, The LORD is with thee, thou mighty man of valour."

THE GENERAL

Congratulations! I have decided who will be promoted to the next rank as my disciple.

THOMAS

What do you mean? What about the training?

THE GENERAL

This *was* the training. And I've decided that my new disciple is … all of you.

THOMAS

What? How is that possible? We are but four fishermen, two tax collectors, five villagers, and a thief!

JUDAS

Hey!

THE GENERAL

And yet you all knew the word well enough to succeed. The application of those scriptures, and a committed and willing heart, is all it takes to become a man in the army of God.

THOMAS

But you said there can only be one?

THE GENERAL

You only succeeded because you all came together as one.

THOMAS

(Crosses arms)
I don't know … sounds fishy.

ALL (EXCEPT THOMAS)

Thomas!

THE GENERAL

Speaking of fishy, I think I deserve some kind of gratitude.
    (Takes fish from bag, returns to men)
Now, let us all bow our heads and—

ALL (EXCEPT THE GENERAL)

Amen!

THE GENERAL

Pray!

THE END

The True Faith

CHARACTERS	ACTORS/ACTRESSES
Christianity	
Islam	
Buddhism	
Wicca	
Hinduism	
Guide	
Stranger	

Guideline

* All character names are centred and in capitals.
* All dialogue is placed under the respective character's name.
* Anything in (brackets) is an action.
* A costume reflecting each respective character is required.

Side Notes

Highlight your parts! Try to remember the line before yours so you know your cue.

Setting

The front of the sanctuary will be where all scenes take place. There will be five seats at the front, one for each belief. The seats will be arranged in a semicircle.

GUIDE

(Enters stage)
This way, please.

STRANGER

(Enters stage)
Where are we?

GUIDE

This is where you make a very important life decision—one that will define you as a person and determine your ultimate outcome.

STRANGER

All in one decision? Sounds kind of heavy, don't you think?

GUIDE

Hey, I don't make the rules. I just address them!

STRANGER

Whatever you say. So what do I do, exactly?

GUIDE

You're going to talk to each of these religious believers and, based on your experience talking to them, determine which belief you want to follow. After you've chosen, I'll reveal what the belief is.

STRANGER

Okay. Who's first?

BUDDHISM

Come here, friend.

STRANGER

(Walks next to Buddhism)

BUDDHISM

(Stands up)

My belief promises peace, tranquillity, and a sense of self.

STRANGER

Whom do you look up to?

BUDDHISM

I have many Gods … but none at all. If you need to know a name, I would say Brahma.

STRANGER

What's in it for you?

BUDDHISM

When I die, I will simply be reincarnated into something far more pleasing to the master.

(Sits down)

GUIDE

What do you think?

STRANGER

I don't know. It sounds kind of boring.

GUIDE

Any particular reason why?

STRANGER

It's way too introspective. I'm not a fan of contemplating my naval all day.

GUIDE

Okay.

(Writes in clipboard)

Next?

HINDUISM

I think I'm next!

STRANGER

(Walks next to Hinduism)

HINDUISM

(Stands up)
My belief promises indulgence, celebrations, and freedom of choice.

STRANGER

Whom do you look up to?

HINDUISM

Well ...
(Ponders and counts)
About 330 million gods.

STRANGER

Are you serious? And you know all their names?

HINDUISM

Oh, no, no. Are you crazy? We're not expected to know all that! We simply
have one for every occasion.

STRANGER

Well, uh, what's in it for you?

HINDUISM

Uh ... I, um ... It can be summed up with ... Well, when I die, I can go to
one of fourteen realms. Then again, that all depends on whether I'm good
or bad in my regular life.
(Sits down)

GUIDE

What do you think?

STRANGER

I don't know. It sounds kind of confusing.

GUIDE

Any particular reason why?

STRANGER

It's way too clustered. I'm not a fan of memorizing things that will only help in very specific situations.

GUIDE

Okay.
    (Writes in clipboard)
Next?

WICCA

If you think you can handle it, step right up.

STRANGER

    (Walks next to Wicca)

WICCA

    (Stands up)
My belief promises exclusivity, euphoria, and oneness with nature.

STRANGER

Whom do you look up to?

WICCA

The Triple Goddess, of course: Maiden, Mother, and Crone.

STRANGER

What's in it for you?

WICCA

I can invoke and conjure healing—and illnesses—to people, if I choose.

                    STRANGER
How often does that work?

                     WICCA
Whenever I believe hard enough.

                    STRANGER
So 10 per cent of the time.

                     WICCA
    (Gasps)
Only because there's a consequence every time it does work. Not that I'd
expect someone like *you* to understand!
    (Sits down)

                     GUIDE
What do you think?

                    STRANGER
I don't know. It sounds kind of hollow.

                     GUIDE
Any particular reason why?

                    STRANGER
It's way too vague. I'm not a fan of wondering whether or not what I'm doing
is right or wrong.

                     GUIDE
Okay.
    (Writes in clipboard)
Next?

                     ISLAM
Over here.

STRANGER

(Walks next to Islam)

ISLAM

(Stands up)
My belief promises peace, elitism, and a feeling of bliss.

STRANGER

Oh, peace? Like the fellow over there?
    (Points at Buddhism)

ISLAM

No! My peace is for me and me alone!

STRANGER

Huh? Whom do you look up to?

ISLAM

Allah is king!

STRANGER

And what's in it for you?

ISLAM

When I die, I will be rewarded with seventy-two virgins!
    (Sits down)

STRANGER

I don't even want to know what that is.

GUIDE

What do you think?

STRANGER

I don't know. It sounds like ... something is missing.

GUIDE

Any particular reason why?

STRANGER

I'm not a fan of blindly following something with no results until death.

GUIDE

Okay.
    (Writes in clipboard)
Last but not least ...

CHRISTIANITY

Hello, how are you?

STRANGER

    (Walks next to Christianity)
Fine, thank you. You're the first one to ask me that all day.

CHRISTIANITY

To God be the glory.

STRANGER

Whom do you look up to?

CHRISTIANITY

I believe in God the Father, God the Son, and God the blessed Holy Ghost.
I believe in the crucifixion. I believe in the blessed trinity, the Godhead,
three in one.

STRANGER

This sounds like an interesting religion.

GUIDE

    (Writes in clipboard)

CHRISTIANITY

I wouldn't call it that. I see it as more of a way of life.

GUIDE

(Crosses out what was written and writes something else in clipboard)

STRANGER

Why's that?

ALL (EXCEPT CHRISTIANITY AND STRANGER)

Please tell us!

CHRISTIANITY

The assurance in knowing that I am fearfully and wonderfully made. The comfort in knowing that I have a God who heals, saves, provides, and delivers me out of harm's way. Not to mention eternal life.

STRANGER

I think I'm ready to choose now! I choose the path that they're on.
    (Points at Christianity)

GUIDE

Pack your things, Buddhism, Hinduism, Wicca, and Islam. Christianity has won today.

CHRISTIANITY

And Christianity is here to stay!

ALL (EXCEPT CHRISTIANITY AND STRANGER)

Wait!

CHRISTIANITY

Yes?

ALL (EXCEPT CHRISTIANITY AND STRANGER)

Um, can we be Christians too?

CHRISTIANITY

Of course. All are welcome. For my God has no biases! Not to age, not to gender, not to race. Remember that Genesis 1:27 says, "God created man in his *own* image, in the image of God created he him; male and female created he them." The God I serve knows that when we stand together ... Well, I'll let Romans 8:37 say the rest!

ALL

(Hold Hands)

"In all these things we are more than conquerors through him that loved us."
    (*Bow*)

CHRISTIANITY

Never forget that you are never too young to serve the Lord, our God!

THE END

The Canvas

CHARACTERS	ACTRESS
Ruth (Insightful)	
Esther (Aristocratic/Realism)	
Deborah (Outspoken/Minimalism)	
Lydia (Diplomatic/Abstractionism)	
Naomi (Depressing/Impressionism)	
Rebekah (Childish/Surrealism)	
Jezebel (Egocentric/Expressionism)	

Guideline

* All character names are centred and in capitals.
* All dialogue is placed under the respective character's name.
* Anything in (brackets) is an action.
* A costume reflecting each respective character is required (e.g., high-class scarf, purse, a jumpsuit, beret)

Side Notes

The words next to the names are their personality traits, as well as their artistic styles. They'll give you an idea on how to act them out. Highlight your parts! Try to remember the line before yours so you know your cue.

Setting

The front of the sanctuary will be where all scenes take place. There will be a canvas on a stand facing away from the audience in the centre of the sanctuary. It will remain so until the end. Around it will be seven chairs, one for each character. The seventh should be slightly separated from the rest; this is where Ruth will sit. Ruth is the only one on stage at the beginning of the play.

Scene 1

RUTH

(Sets up paintbrushes and paint cans by the six main chairs around the canvas)

I can already tell this is going to be great!

ESTHER

(Enters stage gracefully.)

Greetings.

RUTH

(Stops setting up. Rushes away from chairs and towards Esther, to help her to her seat.)

Oh, hello there! You must be …

ESTHER

Esther. Woman of good fortune, nobility, and affluence.

RUTH

You're the first person here.

ESTHER

Punctuality is my formality. Though at times I may excess.

(Directs attention towards a seat.)

May I?

RUTH

Sure.

(Continues setting up.)

ESTHER

I do beg your pardon.

RUTH

(Stops and looks at Esther.)

Oh … I mean, yes, you may.

(Continues setting up.)

ESTHER

You are most kind.

(Takes a seat and begins to fan herself.)

DEBORAH

(Enters stage, searching.)

Hey, you!

RUTH

(Stops setting up.)

Me?

DEBORAH

Yeah, you. Could you help me out with something? See, I'm looking for this painting place, and—

RUTH

(Rushes towards Deborah to help her to her seat.)

You're in the right place. You must be …

DEBORAH

Deborah.

(Stares at Ruth.)

ESTHER

Um. Do tell us a bit more about yourself. So as not to draw any confusion of who you are.

DEBORAH

(Looks at Esther.)

What do you wanna know?

(Curtsies sarcastically.)

Your Highness?

ESTHER

Well, if I may make an observation? Judging by your rather ... brusque response ... I'd say you're outspoken, strong-minded, and courageous.

DEBORAH

Wow.

(Takes a seat.)

I had no idea we'd have a psychic on this job.

RUTH

(Continues setting up.)

Now, now. Let's all try to get along.

LYDIA

(Enters stage quickly.)

Good afternoon, everyone.

(Walks over to Ruth.)

You must be the one in charge.

(Shakes Ruth's hand.)

Pleasure to meet you. My name is Lydia, businesswoman extraordinaire.

(Lets go of Ruth's hand.)

Hard-working, determined, and always hospitable.

DEBORAH

(Sarcastically.)

You forgot modest.

RUTH

Nice to meet you. And I'm not the one in charge—I'm just setting up the paintbrushes.

LYDIA

No need, ma'am. Preparation is key, so I decided to bring my own brushes.
(Takes a seat and pulls out paintbrushes.)

RUTH

All right, I'll just give you the paint, then.
(Continues setting up.)

NAOMI

(Enters stage and sees Ruth.)
Oh, boy.

RUTH

(Sees Naomi, puts everything down, and rushes over to her.)
Naomi!
(Hugs Naomi.)

NAOMI

(Sighs.)
"Call me not Naomi, call me Mara: for the Almighty hath dealt very bitterly
with me."

RUTH

(Looks at Naomi with joy.)
Whatever that means. It's so nice to see a familiar face. Especially one so
joyous, blissful, and pleasant!

NAOMI

Yeah, I'm sure.

RUTH

(Brings Naomi to a seat.)
Come here. Take a seat.
(Sits Naomi down.)
I'll be with you once I finish—

REBEKAH

(Enters stage, twirling.)
Yoo-hoo.

RUTH

Hello there.

REBEKAH

Knock-knock.

RUTH

Who's there?

REBEKAH

Rebekah.

RUTH

Rebekah who?

REBEKAH

The cheerful, simplistic, and most beautiful girl in the world.
(Dances to a seat.)

RUTH

Um, nice to meet you. I'm almost done setting up the paintbrushes, so—

REBEKAH

Paintbrushes? I'm more of a hands-on person when it comes to art.

RUTH

Okay, then. I'll put your painting equipment next to me.
(Finishes setting up and looks at chairs.)
I guess that means there's only one more person left.

DEBORAH
(Looks up at the sky and puts hands together.)
Thank you.

LYDIA
Well, they'd better hurry up. We were supposed to start five minutes ago.

[Music plays.]

JEZEBEL
(Enters stage, posing.)

RUTH
(Rushes over to Jezebel.)
You must be—

JEZEBEL
(Bumps into Ruth.)
Cut, cut! Cut the music!

[Music stops.]

RUTH
That was quite an entrance.

ESTHER
At last. Someone with class.

JEZEBEL
(Looks up and away from everyone.)
Why is this ... peasant ... talking to me?

ESTHER
Perhaps I spoke too soon.

JEZEBEL

(Kisses teeth.)

Now that I, Jezebel, the spitefully cunning mistress of cruelty, am here, you may all introduce yourselves with your name and why you're here.

ESTHER

(Stands up.)

I am—

JEZEBEL

Not going first. I am Jezebel. My specialty is the art of expressionism; it tells the world exactly how you feel about it.

(Takes a seat/)

ESTHER

I am Esther. My specialty is the art of realism, because of its non-subjective reflection of the lives we live.

(Takes a seat.)

DEBORAH

(Stands up.)

Deborah. My specialty is the art of minimalism—small and straight to the point.

(Takes a seat.)

LYDIA

(Stands up.)

My name is Lydia. My specialty is the art of abstractionism; there can always be more than one colourful interpretation.

(Takes a seat.)

NAOMI

(Stands up.)

I'm Nao ... Mara. My specialty is the art of impressionism; specific strokes for specific areas.

(Takes a seat.)

REBEKAH

(Stands up/)
Name's Rebekah! My specialty is the art of surrealism—throw away all
conventional things.
(Takes a seat/)

JEZEBEL

(Waves in Ruth's direction while looking away.)
And you?

RUTH

Me? Oh, uh. I'm no artist. I just work here.

JEZEBEL

Yeah, okay, great. What am I doing here?

Scene 2

RUTH

Well ...
(Takes a seat)
You were all chosen by the leader of this ministry, to take part in a new art
project. One that requires each of your unique and creative talents to—

JEZEBEL

What are we painting?

RUTH

Um ... to be honest, they weren't that specific.

JEZEBEL

(Stands up and walks towards the canvas with paint and brushes in
hand.)
Well, unlike you, I have places to be.
(Begins to visualize a painting.)

ESTHER

(Holds hand out towards Jezebel.)

Ah, ah, ah. Patience is a virtue.

LYDIA

(Stands up and walks towards the canvas with paint and brushes in hand.)

And time is of the essence.

DEBORAH

What's the rush, busybody?

LYDIA

We can't expect things to progress if we just sit on our tushes all day.

NAOMI

Neither can we expect quality from rapid flow of progress.

LYDIA

A-are you doubting my abilities?

ESTHER

Preposterous. She is simply making an observation.

REBEKAH

You talk funny.

ESTHER

I assure you, my art speaks in ways that far surpasses the nature of my vocalizations.

(Stands up and walks towards the canvas.)

Allow me.

REBEKAH

(Looks through Esther's purse.)

LYDIA

(Offers Esther her brush.)

ESTHER

Oh, that won't be necessary. But if you would be so kind as to fetch me my ornaments and tools?

LYDIA

I beg your pardon?

REBEKAH

(Pulls gloves out of Esther's purse.)
Found them!
(Dances to Esther, gives her the gloves and her painting material, and dances back to her seat.)

ESTHER

(Takes gloves and painting material.)
Thank you most sincerely, Rebekah.

LYDIA

Um, those are just gloves.
(Watches Esther.)

ESTHER

(Puts gloves on.)
Excellent observation. Now, if you'll excuse me.
(Begins to paint the canvas.)

JEZEBEL

No, no, no! Excuse me! What are you doing to my canvas?

DEBORAH

Ha! Your canvas?

JEZEBEL

Excuse me! I was talking to Esther.

DEBORAH

Yeah?

NAOMI

Deborah, don't—

DEBORAH

(Stands up)
-And I was talkin' to you.

JEZEBEL

(Looks at Deborah.)
Excuse me!?

RUTH

Ladies, you must come in agreement with your decision making. Why not look at what Esther has done and discuss how you feel about it together?

ALL

(Lean in to look at the canvas.)

JEZEBEL

I don't like it.
(Takes a seat.)

DEBORAH

(Sarcastically.)
Off to a great start.
(Takes a seat.)

LYDIA

At least it is a start.
(Takes a seat.)

NAOMI

Esther.

ESTHER

(Stops painting.)
Yes, Naomi?

NAOMI

Please call me Mara. I was wondering, why that colour?

ESTHER

I admire your curiosity.
   (Takes a seat.)
The answer lies in Psalms 23:1–2.

REBEKAH

(Stands up.)
"The LORD is my shepherd; I shall not want. He maketh me to lie down in
green pastures: he leadeth me beside the still waters." You're welcome.
   (Sits down.)

RUTH

Ah, I see. You used the scripture to give you an idea. Very clever.

LYDIA

I still don't see why you needed gloves, and a different set of brushes for that.

DEBORAH

(Sarcastically.)
Obviously, your brushes weren't good enough for Her Majesty.

ESTHER

Deborah, again with such hostility?

DEBORAH

Just making an observation. So, queeny, please do tell us why you—

JEZEBEL
(Stands up.)
Wrong, all wrong! All of it wrong, wrong, wrong! Esther, speaking from personal experience, I know for a fact that pastors aren't green.

REBEKAH
Open your ears, Jezebel. It says pastures, not pastors.

JEZEBEL
Oh ... Carry on.
(Sits down.)

REBEKAH
You're welcome.

RUTH
Why don't you all take pointers from Esther and use the scriptures to your advantage?

NAOMI
Then what will we do about the colours orange and pink?

LYDIA
Simple: don't use them.

DEBORAH
(Stands up with painting tools and walks towards the canvas.)

ESTHER
And thus, the artistic urges take play.

DEBORAH
(Begins painting.)
Don't think it has anything to do with you, Esther. This is between me and God.

ESTHER

And God has delivered you from your unsociable demeanour.

DEBORAH

Yeah? What makes you so sure?

LYDIA

You just called her Esther.

ESTHER

An excellent observation, Lydia.

DEBORAH

I'm not seeing your point here.
   (Stops painting.)

RUTH

Well, I for one am happy to see you coming out of your agitating shell, Deborah. And I'd be even happier if we all took a look at what Deborah has contributed.

ALL

   (Lean in to look at the canvas.)

REBEKAH

Um. Am I the only one not seeing anything?

JEZEBEL

She obviously forgot to put paint on the brush. Rookie mistake.

NAOMI

No, I think I see something.

RUTH

Naomi's right.

NAOMI

Mara!

RUTH

Look closer. Deborah, would you mind telling us what you added?

DEBORAH

You see, I took my inspiration from Psalms 68:13, which says—

REBEKAH

(Stands up.)
Which says, "Though ye have lien among the pots, yet shall ye be as the wings of a dove covered with *silver*, and her feathers with *yellow gold*."

ALL

(Look at Rebekah.)

REBEKAH

(Looks at everyone.)
You're welcome.
(Sits down.)

LYDIA

(Looks at painting.)
So you painted a dove's feathers?

JEZEBEL

Ha! Looks more like a malnourished zebra.

DEBORAH

(Angrily.)
Actually, it's minimalist art—something I doubt you'd understand.
(Marches towards Jezebel.)
But I'm more than willing to teach you about it.

RUTH

(Stands and stops Deborah.)

"A fool's wrath is presently known: but a prudent *man* covereth shame."
Proverbs 12:16.

DEBORAH

I'm not a man.

JEZEBEL

You could have fooled me.

DEBORAH

When I get my hands on you ...!

(Attempts to go past Ruth.)

NAOMI

(Helps Ruth by standing up and pulling Deborah back to her seat.)

"The beginning of strife is as when one letteth out water: therefore leave off
contention, before it be meddled with." Proverbs 17:14.

DEBORAH

(Looks at Naomi, sighs, and takes a seat.)

NAOMI

(Looks at Jezebel.)

If you're so clever, why don't you—

JEZEBEL

(Stands up with painting tools and drops scarf.)

Show you all how a real artist paints? Watch me.

(Walks towards the canvas and begins painting.)

ESTHER

You need not be hasty, Jezebel.

JEZEBEL

And you need not distract me, princess.

ESTHER

Princess? You are mistaken. I am—

JEZEBEL

Distorting my focus.

ESTHER

My sincerest apologies. I simply meant—

JEZEBEL

Shh! The queen is painting.

ESTHER

(Gasps.)
You fancy yourself a monarch?

JEZEBEL

I am quite fancy, aren't I?

ESTHER

(Stands up and walks to Jezebel.)
Absurd! You are no less than a ... a megalomaniac.

JEZEBEL

(Stops painting and looks up.)
Excuse me, princess. I am trying to paint here, unlike the rest of you. All
you've managed to do is taint my beautiful canvas.

ALL (EXCEPT JEZEBEL)

Excuse me?

ESTHER

(Holds gloved hand out.)

NAOMI

(Takes off Esther's glove, lightly hits Jezebel's shoulder with it, returns glove to Esther, and sits down.)

ESTHER

(Sits down.)

JEZEBEL

After all my hard work, you repay me with a hit on the shoulder? That's it.
    (Drops paint supplies.)
I'm leaving. You can paint this yourselves.
    (Exits stage.)

RUTH

Oh, no. Her portion wasn't completed.

LYDIA

No big deal. I can finish it so long as I know what exactly she was trying to make.

NAOMI

It looks like some sort of …

ALL

(Lean in to look at the canvas.)

RUTH

Some sort of colourful linen around the edges?

REBEKAH

Oh
    (Stands up.)
"And thou shalt make an hanging for the door of the tent, of *blue*, and *purple*, and *scarlet*, and fine twined linen, wrought with needlework." Exodus 26:36. You're welcome.

DEBORAH

Oh, I'm starting to see it now.

REBEKAH

You're welcome!

ESTHER

A very remarkable choice on her behalf.

REBEKAH

I said, you're welcome!
        (Sits down.)
Ugh, you guys never appreciate what I have to say.

LYDIA

Okay, I suggest that Naomi, Rebekah, and I complete the scarlet, blue, and purple linen, respectively. That way by the time we each finish, we'll have the painting done in its entirety.

RUTH

That sounds like a great idea, Lydia!

REBEKAH

Yeah, great idea, Lydia.
        (Swaps paint cans.)

LYDIA

All right, ladies, let's begin.

NAOMI & REBEKAH
        (Stand up with painting tools and walk towards the canvas.)

LYDIA

Ruth, do you mind handing me my paint can?

RUTH

Sure thing.
        (Stand up with Lydia's paint can and walks towards the canvas.)
Wait, something seems wrong.
        (Looks inside Lydia's paint can.)

LYDIA

Don't be ridiculous. Just hand it here.
        (Grabs paint can.)

RUTH

        (Pulls paint can back.)
Lydia, wait. This isn't what you think it is.

LYDIA

Just give it here so we can finish the painting.
        (Pulls paint can back.)

RUTH

No, wait! You don't understand!
        (Paint can slips out of hand, and paint lands on the canvas)

ALL

        (Stand up if not already standing.)
No!

LYDIA

White paint? Really, Ruth? I asked for my paint can! You know, the one with purple in it?

RUTH

I tried telling you—

LYDIA

You should have looked before carelessly handing it to me. Could you be any more unprofessional?

(Takes all personal belongings.)

I've had it. I'm leaving! Call me when we've got a more responsible team working on this project.

(Exits stage.)

DEBORAH

And to think I put in all that effort for nothing.

(Takes all personal belongings and exits stage.)

ESTHER

Deborah and Jezebel's portions could be replicated without struggle. It is my portion that received the harshest of punishments.

(Takes all personal belongings.)

Alas, I must be on my way.

(Curtsies to Ruth and exits stage.)

REBEKAH

(Cunningly.)

Oh? Is it time to leave already?

(Exits stage.)

NAOMI

(Begins to leave.)

RUTH

You too, Naomi?

NAOMI

It's M ... never mind. I'm sorry to do this to you, Ruth.

(Exits stage.)

RUTH

How could you all just leave like this?

(Sighs and looks up.)

Lord, I know I'm not an artist, or painter, or anything of the sort, but I have to finish this painting.

(Looks at canvas.)

As Philippians 4:13 says …

(Picks up painting tools.)

"I can do all things through Christ who strengthens me."

(Begins to paint.)

Scene 3

[After sixteen seconds, the music plays.]

JEZEBEL

(Enters stage posing, goes over to her seat.)

All right, cut the music!

[Music Stops]

RUTH

(Still painting.)

I couldn't help but notice you come in, Jezebel.

JEZEBEL

As if I came for *you.* I'm here because I forgot my scarf.

(Puts scarf on and shows off to Ruth.)

It's real cashmere, you know.

(Sees Ruth's painting and screams.)

NAOMI

(Enters stage.)

I heard a scream. Are you okay, Ruth?

JEZEBEL

Excuse me! Aren't you forgetting someone?

NAOMI

Jezebel? You came back?

RUTH

(Still painting.)
She forgot her scarf, but now that she has it, I'm sure she'll be right on her way home. Isn't that right, Jezebel?

JEZEBEL

What are you doing to my beautiful art?

RUTH

One might say I'm fine-tuning it.

NAOMI

Fine-tuning?
(Looks at painting and is surprised.)
Ruth, this is … this is …

JEZEBEL

Ruined beyond repair!

REBEKAH

(Enters stage.)
Did something happen while I was away? I heard a loud noise.
(Sees Ruth's painting.)
Whoa! What is that? It looks like it's …

JEZEBEL

Sabotaged! Incapacitated!

ESTHER

(Enters stage.)
Such harsh words are quite unbefitting of a lady!
(Sees Ruth's painting.)
But such elegance could only be the product of one! Is that …?

JEZEBEL

The last thing you ever do, so long as I live?

DEBORAH

(Enters stage.)
And how long is that, exactly? 'Cause if it goes on any longer, I might
have to …
(Sees Ruth's painting.)
Call the press, 'cause you just made history. This is totally …

JEZEBEL

Juvenile! Unprofessional!

LYDIA

(Enters stage.)
I'll be the judge of that.
(Sees Ruth's painting.)
Amazing. What is it?

RUTH

(Stops painting.)
It's done!
(Turns painting towards the audience.)

LYDIA

Surely I must have … inspired you in some way.

DEBORAH

Says the girl who didn't even touch the canvas. Let's face it: she couldn't have
done the centre like that without my handiwork.

ESTHER

Are you referring to your rather dreary arrangement of lines? The green was undoubtedly of my doing.

REBEKAH

But I gave her the white paint that spilled on the canvas in the first place!

ALL (EXCEPT REBEKAH)
(Look at Rebekah.)

REBEKAH

I mean … never mind.

NAOMI

Everyone, back up! Since Ruth is the one that finished it, I think she should decide who gets the credit.

RUTH

Thank you, Naomi.

NAOMI

You're welcome, Ruth.

RUTH

As for who should get the credit …

ALL (EXCEPT RUTH)
(Lean in to hear Ruth.)

RUTH

I believe all credit is due to the Father.

ALL (EXCEPT RUTH)

Yes?

RUTH

The Son.

ALL (EXCEPT RUTH)

Yes?

RUTH

And the blessed Holy Ghost.

ALL

Amen!

THE END

Rogues Gallery

CHARACTERS	ACTORS/ACTRESSES
Jordan King (The Superior)	
Jirah Spalton (The Rebel)	
Frankincense "Franky" Knox (The Jock)	
Betharam "Beth" Henderson (The Princess)	
Asher Adams (The Hustler)	
Penelope Legume (The Outcast)	
Mr. Moreh (The Teacher)	

Guideline

* All character names are centred and in capitals.
* All dialogue is placed under the respective character's name.
* Anything in (brackets) is an action.
* A costume reflecting each respective character is required (e.g., long-sleeved undershirt, leatherjacket, letterman jacket, high-end fashion, trench coat, school uniform)

Side Notes

The words next to the names are their personality traits. They'll give you an idea on how to act them out. Highlight your parts! Try to remember the line before yours so you know your cue.

Setting

The front of the sanctuary will be where all scenes take place. There will be seven chairs on stage, and every character gets one. Franky and Mr. Moreh are the only two characters not already on stage. All characters begin sitting at a distance from each other.

FRANKY
(Enters stage and sees ASHER.)

ASHER & FRANKY
Bom-bom!
(Rush to each other, clap-clap-hug-snap.)

FRANKY
Sup, bruddah?

ASHER
S'all good, man. You know how I do.

FRANKY
Still dealing those school supplies, Asher?

ASHER
Yeah, man. How do you think I got here?
(Checks supplies.)
Whatchu need?

FRANKY
What I need is to get out of this detention. Know what I mean? Who even goes to school on a Sunday?

ASHER
Don't worry, I gotchu. This detention will be over before you can say "laboraioz."

JORDAN
It's pronounced laborious.

ASHER
Huh?

FRANKY

What?

ASHER

You hear somethin'?

JORDAN

Of course not. The only words you can hear are protein shake and contraband.

FRANKY

(Looks around.)
Where?

JIRAH

Wow.

ASHER

(Laughs and walks over to Jirah.)
I've been called many things by the ladies: suave, and romantic. But wow? Hmm …
(Winks at Jirah.)
I think I could get used to it.

JIRAH

(Backs away.)
Ha! You wish.

ASHER

Upon a star. You into astronomy?

JORDAN

Astrology!

ASHER

Geography. I'm a Sagittarius. What's your sign?

JIRAH
(Nods head and smiles sarcastically.)
Stop!

FRANKY
(Still searching.)
Where's my protein shake?

JORDAN
Wherever you left your brain today.

FRANKY
Who said that?
(Walks over to Beth.)
Was it you?

BETH
(Trying to hide her face with a hat.)
Um, no! It wasn't me …

FRANKY
I can't hear you with that hat on.
(Takes off Beth's hat.)

BETH
How could you?

JIRAH
(Looks at Beth and snarks.)
No way! Beth Henderson? Little miss perfect everything!
(Laughs.)
How the mighty have fallen.

ASHER
Wait, you never get in trouble for anything here!

JIRAH

I thought rich ol' mommy and daddy would just pay teachers to keep quiet about any of your ... misconduct.

BETH

(Stands up.)
I didn't do anything wrong!

JIRAH

Hey, hey, take it easy, princess. No one's blaming you for your bleak sense of style.

ASHER & FRANKY

Ooo!

BETH

Heh. What would you know about style? I'm the leader of the fashion club, the design club, the hair stylist committee, the yearbook ...
(Looks at Jirah.)
You're just a girl who blames all her problems on everyone but herself. And your jacket is *so* three decades ago.

JIRAH

(Walks over to Beth.)
What'd you say about my jacket, you little Barbie doll?

BETH

Barbie doll? Really? You're comparing me to a Barbie doll?

JIRAH

Cheap, artificial, brainless—I'd say it's pretty accurate.

ASHER &FRANKY

Ooo!

BETH

About as accurate as your clothing coordination. [Insert Jirah's clothing here]? Did you even try this morning?

JIRAH

Harder than you did, miss [insert Beth's clothing here]. Oh, yeah, I talk the talk too, princess.

ASHER &FRANKY

Cat fight! Cat fight! Cat fight!

JIRAH & BETH

(Slowly return to their seats, looking at each other with disgust.)

ASHER & FRANKY

Aw …

JORDAN

Can we at least try to act like we're high school students and not ten-year-olds?

ASHER

(Taps Franky's shoulder.)
Yo, Franky. I think I heard it that time.

FRANKY

(Smiles.)
So I'm not just hearing voices!
(Looks around the room.)
Oh, there you are.
(Walks toward Jordan.)

JORDAN

(Stands up.)
Finally seeing clearly now, are we?

FRANKY
(Walks past Jordan and goes to Penelope.)
I could barely hear you over there.

JORDAN
(Shakes head and sits down.)
Why do I even bother?

FRANKY

What are you in for?

PENELOPE
(Looks up at Franky and quickly looks away.)

ASHER

Can't be anything serious. She's one of those quiet, shy-girl types. Never talks in class, never gets in fights, never eats with people.

JIRAH

And why do you know this?

ASHER

I know everything that goes down in this school, sweetheart.

JORDAN

Perks of being a felon.

ASHER

Whoa, whoa. I ain't no felon.

JORDAN

Explain all the knockoff school supplies you sell in that trench coat of yours.

ASHER

Yo! I don't sell knockoffs …
    (Looks at audience and smiles.)
I sell replicas.

JORDAN

Is that why you're in here?

ASHER

All information on purchases, and the result of such, are strictly confidential.

JORDAN

Wow, where'd you learn such big words?

ASHER

When it comes to business, I try to be air-tight.

JORDAN

You mean erudite?

ASHER

Man … You know what I mean.

PENELOPE

    (Looks at everyone with anger.)
I tried to jump off a roof!

ALL (EXCEPT PENELOPE)
    (Stares at Penelope in silence.)

MR. MOREH

    (Enters stage.)

JORDAN

Oh, thank goodness you're here! There seems to be a misunderstanding, I
don't belong—

MR. MOREH

Hello, everyone.

FRANKY

Wait, you're not the detention supervisor.

MR. MOREH

I know. They called in sick, so I was asked to be here. What do they usually do?

ASHER

(Stands up and smiles.)
They usually let us go home around this time.

MR. MOREH

Ah, ah, ah. Proverbs 12:22 says, "Lying lips are abomination to the Lord: but they that deal truly are his delight."

FRANKY

And ... you're a Christian.

JORDAN

Well, this *is* a predominantly Christian school.

FRANKY

It is?
(Looks around the room.)
That explains so much!

JIRAH

(Looks up.)
Father, you've gotta be kiddin'.

MR. MOREH

Exodus 20:7 says, "Thou shalt not take the name of the LORD thy God in vain; for the LORD will not hold him guiltless that taketh his name in vain."

JIRAH

Ha. Is that all you're here to do? Tell us what we're doing wrong and how to fix it, so we're all better people by the end of the day?

MR. MOREH

That sounds like a great idea!

ALL (EXCEPT MR. MOREH & JIRAH)

Aw, man!

JIRAH

(Walks towards Mr. Moreh.)
Wait, I was just kidding around.

MR. MOREH

And now that you're standing around, you can go first, Miss …
(Takes a seat.)

JIRAH

(Sigh.)
Spalton. Jirah Spalton.
What do you wanna know?

ASHER

(Raises hand.)
I wanna know—

JIRAH

Oh, no, you don't!

FRANKY

What're you in for?

JIRAH

The worst thing ever! Teachers started calling my house, telling my parents that I haven't been showing up lately. My parents, being the high and mighty corporate suits they are, yelled at me—big surprise there. They started saying things like, "You're a disappointment. You're a disgrace. You couldn't graduate if your life depended on it." You know, the usual stuff. So, I decided to prove 'em wrong by showing up and getting my marks up. But the teacher kept hounding me, asking me questions I obviously wouldn't know unless I showed up those weeks I skipped, you know? After a while, I couldn't take it anymore. I stood up and gave the teacher what he had coming to 'em.

ALL (EXCEPT JIRAH)

You punched the teacher?

JIRAH

You really think I'd still be at this school if I did that? I didn't punch him. I just gave him a piece of my mind. I said, "Look, if you're going to pick on me all day, I suggest you meet me after class, where I don't use words to fight my battles." I don't see what I did wrong.

JORDAN

Uh, You threatened a teacher.

JIRAH

I was just defending myself.

MR. MOREH

Ephesians 4:29 says, "Let no corrupt communication proceed out of your mouth, but that which is good to the use of edifying, that it may minister grace unto the hearers."

JIRAH

(Shakes head.)

You don't get it! Everyone is always against me! The one time I try to fight back, I get in more trouble. I never win!

MR. MOREH

(Stands up.)

Deuteronomy 31:6 states, "Be strong and of a good courage, fear not, nor be afraid of them: for the Lord thy God, he it is that doth go with thee; he will not fail thee, nor forsake thee."

JIRAH

(Sighs and sits down.)

FRANKY

I mean ... I think he has a point, Jirah.

MR. MOREH

Would you like to be next, Mister ...?

FRANKY

Knox.

(Stands up.)

Franky Knox. Quarterback, captain of three sports teams, and one of them is football.

JORDAN

(Sarcastically.)

Really? I had no idea.

FRANKY

I'm only here because my marks haven't been on the good side lately. I've been way too busy with my actual goal in life: to become a professional player in the big leagues. And last time I checked, I don't need good marks to be a good player.

MR. MOREH

Romans 12:2 says, "And be not conformed to this world: but be ye transformed by the renewing of your mind, that ye may prove what *is* that good, and acceptable, and perfect, will of God."

FRANKY

But—

BETH

(Tries to sneak out.)

MR. MOREH

Ecclesiastes 7:12 reads, "For wisdom *is* a defence, *and* money *is* a defence: but the excellency of knowledge *is, that* wisdom giveth life to them that have it."

FRANKY

What about—

MR. MOREH

Proverbs 16:16 states, "How much better *is it* to get wisdom than gold! and to get understanding rather to be chosen than silver!" Need I say more?

FRANKY

I take that back, Jirah!
 (Sits down.)

MR. MOREH

Where do you think you're going?

BETH

(Startled.)
How did you know?

MR. MOREH

Care to tell us why you're in such a rush to leave, Miss ...?

BETH

(Sighs and walks to the front.)
Henderson. Beth Henderson. I have a mani-pedi in ten minutes so I have to go!

JIRAH

(Sarcastically.)

No, please. Tell us your oh-so-interesting story.

BETH

When I was ten everything was what—

JORDAN

How'd you get in detention, Beth?

BETH

Oh ... right. It wasn't my fault! No, really it wasn't! I was with my friends at school, and this girl walked by. I felt kind of sorry for her at first. She looked like one of those awkward, quirky, introverts that every teenager without an actual personality pretends to be. Head firmly in her book. My friends started laughing at her, so I laughed with them. When she walked in front of us, she tripped on my foot. It wasn't my fault.

PENELOPE

And what did you do to her after she fell?

BETH

I don't know. I think I just walked away or something. I was afraid of what she might do.

PENELOPE

(Stands up.)

Don't you remember throwing my books out a window?

BETH

Uh, kind of ... Wait that was you?

MR. MOREH

Beth, 2 Timothy 1:7 says, " For God hath not given us the spirit of fear; but of power, and of love, and of a sound mind."

BETH

How was it my fault? My friends should be in detention too!

PENELOPE

(Walks over to Beth, pushing her to her seat.)
They didn't trip me on purpose! They didn't throw out my books! They didn't drive me to suicide.

BETH

(Sits down.)
Suicide?

PENELOPE

Yes! I recognized three of you as soon as I got here!
(Points at Beth.)
You bullied me all day!
(Points at Asher.)
You stole my books after they were thrown out the window.
(Points at Jordan.)
And you pulled the fire alarm before I could jump.

ASHER

Hey, now! All information on purchases, and how I got them in the first place, are strictly confidential.

JORDAN

And I'm in detention because I saved your life by pulling that fire alarm.

MR. MOREH

Okay, one at a time. Penelope Legume, Matthew 5:43 reads, "Ye have heard that it hath been said, Thou shalt love thy neighbour, and hate thine enemy. But I say unto you, Love your enemies, bless them that curse you, do good to them that hate you, and pray for them which despitefully use you, and persecute you." Asher Adams, Ephesians 4:28 says, "Let him that stole steal no more: but rather let him labour, working with his hands the thing which is good, that he may have to give to him that needeth." And Jordan King,

Proverbs 11:2 tells us, "When pride cometh, then cometh shame: but with the lowly is wisdom."

ALL (EXCEPT MR. MOREH)
(Sit down if not already seated.)
You know our names?

MR. MOREH
Of course. I am a Sunday school teacher, after all. Well, that and …
(Turns clipboard around.)
This has your names on it.

JIRAH
Then why'd you make us introduce ourselves?

MR. MOREH
Simple. I wanted to know if you knew who you were. Jordan, your name is the chief river of Palestine, where many biblical events take place. Jirah, your name is related to Jireh, as in the Lord will provide. Franky—or should I say Frankincense, one of the consecrated incenses used in both the Old and New Testaments. Beth—or should I say Betharam, one of the cities alotted by Moses to Gad? Asher, your name is that of the second son of Jacob and Zilpah, who shall yield royal dainties. Penelope, your surname Legume is important because it is one of the earliest plants in the region.

ALL (EXCEPT MR. MOREH)
What's your name?

MR. MOREH
I am Mr. Moreh. As in, many plains with trees and mountains. It is also the Hebrew translation for a male teacher.
(Looks at watch and starts walking.)
Which reminds me, I should get going. I have to return to my church.

PENELOPE
Wait! Thank you for everything.

MR. MOREH

Don't thank me—thank God. You guys created the scene; God gave me the scriptures you needed to hear. All that's left is for one of you to read 1 Peter 3:8–9.

(Smiles at audience and continues walking.)

I think my work here is done.

JORDAN

(Stands up.)

A scripture for every situation. And here I thought I was here by mistake.

JIRAH

(Stands up.)

I guess sometimes there are no mistakes. Everything has to happen for a reason, you know?

FRANKY

(Stands up.)

Study to show ourselves approved. Yo, Ash, can you find that scripture for me?

(Walks over to Asher and takes Bible out of his trench coat.)

BETH

(Stands up.)

We should be looking for 1 Peter 3:8–9—and apologizing for what we've done wrong.

ASHER

(Stands up.)

I found it! 1 Peter 3:8–9. I think it'd be best if you read it, Penelope.

PENELOPE

(Stands up and takes the Bible.)

Thank you. "Finally, be ye all of one mind, having compassion one of another, love as brethren, be pitiful, be courteous: Not rendering evil for evil, or railing for railing: but contrariwise blessing; knowing that ye are thereunto called, that ye should inherit a blessing."

THE END

The Third Dimension

Characters	Actor/Actresses
Moses (Honourable Fasting)	
Jabez (Peaceful Praying)	
Hezekiah (Wise Reading)	
Gideon (Faithful Applying)	
Samson (Strong Loving)	
Being in White	
The Voice of the Wilderness	

Guideline

* All character names are centred and in capitals.
* All dialogue is placed under the respective character's name.
* Anything in (brackets) is an action.
* A costume reflecting each respective character is required (e.g., different coloured T-shirts, travelling bags)

Side Notes

The words next to the names are personality traits and key moments to remember them by in this play. They'll give you an idea on how to act them out. Highlight your parts! Try to remember the line before yours so you know your cue. When "TIME PASSES BY," the actors are required to show the actions they've been doing while time passed. All of these "TIME PASSES BY" scenes end with the actors asleep. The Voice of the Wilderness should never be seen, only heard.

Setting

The wilderness. The front of the sanctuary will be where all scenes take place. There will be a door facing towards the audience, in the centre of the sanctuary. It will remain there until the end. The Being in White is behind the door at the beginning of the play.

BEING IN WHITE

"The voice of him that crieth in the wilderness, Prepare ye the way of the LORD, make straight in the desert a highway for our God. Every valley shall be exalted, and every mountain and hill shall be made low: and the crooked shall be made straight, and the rough places plain: And the glory of the LORD shall be revealed, and all flesh shall see it together: for the mouth of the LORD hath spoken it." Isaiah 40:3–5.

(Goes behind door to exit stage.)

ALL (EXCEPT BEING IN WHITE)

(Enter stage, walking through the aisle.)

MOSES

Men! We finally made it!

GIDEON

Where exactly is it?

HEZEKIAH

You've been travelling all this way without a clue?

SAMSON

You really expect someone like him to know? Ha! But really, where is it?

JABEZ

Be nice, guys. We're in a place of grace.

ALL (EXCEPT BEING IN WHITE)

(Arrive at the front of the sanctuary.)

MOSES

Here we are! Deep within the wilderness! To God be the glory.

SAMSON

Yes. But you still haven't explained why you brought us here.

HEZEKIAH

It was in the wilderness that many received their close relationship with the Lord.

GIDEON

I see. So this trip is to build on our spiritual foundation?

MOSES

My brother, it is much more than that! It's been a long travel. I suggest we rest before we do anything else.

JABEZ

Great idea, but first we should pray!

MOSES

Right on. Would anyone like to do the honours?
(Looks around.)

ALL (EXCEPT JABEZ)

(Look away so as not to be selected.)

JABEZ

(Raises hand excitingly.)

MOSES

(Unaware of Jabez.)
Really, men? We've come all this way, travelled for seven days with nothing but the clothes on our back and the food in our bags, and no one is willing to pray?

GIDEON

(Points to Jabez.)
Well, since he suggested it, shouldn't he pray?

MOSES

(Looks at Jabez.)

I guess it's only fair. They say you can tell a lot about someone by the way he prays. Since you're the newest and the youngest one here, your prayer should be genuine. May we come in agreement with his prayer.

ALL

(Bow heads and pray.)

JABEZ

Oh, that thou wouldest bless me indeed, and enlarge my coast, and that thine hand might be with me, and that thou wouldest keep *me* from evil, that it may not grieve me! Amen.

ALL (EXCEPT JABEZ)

Amen!

MOSES

Sleep well, everyone.

ALL

(Rest their heads on the floor.)

THE VOICE OF THE WILDERNESS

Behold. My children are resting outside my door. They have been pressing with a purpose in the gospel. So they now desire to enter the third dimension in the Holy Spirit. I send thou, my messenger, to go before the leader among them and reveal to him what must be done to receive the gifts they desire.

BEING IN WHITE

I shall.

(Enters stage from behind door.)

Moses. Moses.

(Walks over to Moses.)

Moses!

MOSES

(Wakes up.)

Ah! I had a wild dream. In it, I was walking around with people for forty years, and no matter what I did, they wouldn't listen.

(Shakes head.)

You must be the messenger.

BEING IN WHITE

Indeed, I am. The Lord has sent me to tell you that your heart's desire for the third dimension in the Holy Spirit lies behind this door. But you and your men may enter if—and only if—you make the sacrifices required.

MOSES

Praise Jehovah! I will do my best. What is it that we require?

BEING IN WHITE

The fruits of the earth will soon be forgotten; without any nurturing, they will grow rotten. The fruits of the Spirit will set you free, so hold strong together in harmony.

MOSES

What?

(Looks away to think.)

BEING IN WHITE

Fear not, for the Lord thy God will be with you through it all.

(Exits behind door.)

MOSES

Fruits of the Spirit …

(Scratches beard.)

Men, wake up. Wake up!

ALL (EXCEPT MOSES)

(Wake up slowly, but stay on the ground)

Ugh!

MOSES

The messenger of the Lord appeared before me. He brought to my attention that we must present our bodies as a living sacrifice. What better way to do that than by fasting!

ALL (EXCEPT MOSES)

Aw!

MOSES

Uh, uh! Let's not forget Matthew 6:16–18 says, "Moreover when ye fast, be not, as the hypocrites, of a sad countenance: for they disfigure their faces, that they may appear unto men to fast. Verily I say unto you, They have their reward. But thou, when thou fastest, anoint thine head, and wash thy face; That thou appear not unto men to fast, but unto thy Father which is in secret: and thy Father, which seeth in secret, shall reward thee openly."

SAMSON

(Stands up.)
Well, we can't argue with that. Wait a minute. Who's Matthew, Moses?

MOSES

Don't worry, Samson.
(Looks at audience)
They know who I'm talking about.

SAMSON

(Points at Hezekiah.)
You're the smart one here. Any suggestion for our fasting length?

HEZEKIAH

(Stands up and thinks.)
Hmm …
(Walks around, thinking.)
Jesus gave seven parables. He also performed seven miracles on the Holy Sabbath Day. There are seven days in the week. We shall fast for seven days!

MOSES

Then it is settled! We shall fast for seven days, in hopes that we will be granted entrance into the third dimension in the Holy Spirit.

THE VOICE OF THE WILDERNESS

(Sings "God Has Not Forgot.")

(TIME PASSES BY)

MOSES

(Looks to make sure everyone is asleep. Tries to open the door, but it is still locked. Goes back to sleep.)

THE VOICE OF THE WILDERNESS

(Stops singing.)

Behold. My youths have fasted with a seeking heart for my gifts. Yet the spirit indeed *is* willing, but the flesh is still weak. I send thou, my messenger, to go before the youngest of them. I have heard his cries. Give him a message of hope and of guidance.

BEING IN WHITE

I shall.

(Enters stage from behind door.)

Jabez, Jabez! You are not the pain you were so named. Jabez!

JABEZ

(Wakes up and stands.)

A messenger does appear before me?

BEING IN WHITE

And a door lies between us.

JABEZ

But what lies behind this door?

BEING IN WHITE

The third dimension in the Holy Spirit. More than an infilling, but a new beginning.

JABEZ

Messenger of the Lord, tempt me not. Advise me of the key's location.

BEING IN WHITE

I tempt you not. The key lies within you all, for Jesus left the power here.
(Points before them and pauses.)
Your hands command a great authority. It's placed there by one, but meant for the majority. You fast as a body, your bellies did speak, but in your hands lie the answers you seek.

JABEZ

I, uh …
(Looks away to think.)

BEING IN WHITE

Fear not, for the Lord thy God will be with you through it all.
(Exits behind door.)

JABEZ

Great authority … in my hands?
(Thinks hard.)
Men, wake up. Wake up!

ALL (EXCEPT JABEZ)

(Wake up slowly, but stay on the ground.)
Ugh!

JABEZ

The messenger of the Lord appeared before me.

MOSES

You too? What did he say?

JABEZ

I think he wants us to pray along with our fast … for another seven days.

ALL (EXCEPT JABEZ AND MOSES)

Aw!

JABEZ

Oh, come on, men! Don't you remember Philippians 4:6–7? "Be careful for nothing; but in every thing by prayer and supplication with thanksgiving let your requests be made known unto God. And the peace of God, which passeth all understanding, shall keep your hearts and minds through Christ Jesus."

SAMSON

Well, we can't argue with that.

MOSES

Amen! We shall pray along with our fast for another seven days, in hopes that we will be granted entrance into the third dimension in the Holy Spirit.

THE VOICE OF THE WILDERNESS
(Sings "There Is Power in the Name of Jesus.")
(TIME PASSES BY)

JABEZ
(Looks to make sure everyone is asleep, then tries to open the door. It is still locked. Goes back to sleep.)

THE VOICE OF THE WILDERNESS
(Stops singing.)
Behold. My people have fasted and prayed with a seeking heart for my gifts. Yet still the Spirit indeed is willing, but the flesh is weak. I send thou, my messenger, to go before the studious one among them. Give him a message of wisdom beyond his own understanding.

BEING IN WHITE

I shall.

(Enters stage from behind door.)

Hezekiah! You have waited for my call, and here I am. Hezekiah, awake from this slumber. Hezekiah!

HEZEKIAH

(Wakes up, stands, and points at BEING IN WHITE.)

Messenger?

(Points at door.)

Door? You must be who the other two were talking about.

BEING IN WHITE

Aye, I have been sent here by the will of the Lord thy God to deliver a message.

HEZEKIAH

Okay, let me hear it.

BEING IN WHITE

Two pieces were solved, but three do remain. The word of the Lord is for you to maintain. Plain text on a page can be useless or odd, but there's no greater text than the scriptures of God.

HEZEKIAH

(Snaps fingers.)

Ha! This one is easy!

BEING IN WHITE

Fear not …

(Looks at Hezekiah with a smile.)

Fear not, for the Lord thy God will be with you through it all.

(Exits behind door.)

HEZEKIAH

Indeed, I do believe. Men, wake up. Wake up!

ALL (EXCEPT HEZEKIAH)
(Wake up slowly, but stay on the ground.)
Ugh!

HEZEKIAH

The messenger of the Lord, the same one that appeared before Moses and Jabez, appeared before me. He's telling us to not only fast and pray, but to also read the Word.

GIDEON

Let me guess: another seven days?

HEZEKIAH

You'd better believe it. And before anyone groans, let's hold closely to 2 Timothy 3:16–17. "All scripture is given by inspiration of God, and is profitable for doctrine, for reproof, for correction, for instruction in righteousness: That the man of God may be perfect, thoroughly furnished unto all good works."

MOSES

Amen! We shall read the Word along with our fasting and prayer for another seven days, in hopes that we will be granted entrance into the third dimension in the Holy Spirit.

THE VOICE OF THE WILDERNESS
(Sings "Holy Spirit Rain Down.")
(TIME PASSES BY)

HEZEKIAH
(Looks to make sure everyone is asleep, tries to open the door. It is still locked. Goes back to sleep.)

THE VOICE OF THE WILDERNESS
(Stops singing.)
Behold. My kin have fasted, prayed, and read my Word with a seeking heart for my gifts. Yet still the Spirit is willing, but the flesh is weak. I send thou,

my messenger, to go before the inquisitive one among them. Give him a message of truth and deliverance.

BEING IN WHITE

I shall.
(Enters stage from behind door.)
Gideon!

GIDEON

(Wakes up, stands.)
Yes! I have been waiting for your message.

BEING IN WHITE

To God be the glory, I am here. To give you a message from the Lord thy God.

GIDEON

Show me!

BEING IN WHITE

I ... I beg your pardon?

GIDEON

Show me that you are a messenger of the Lord first. Then I will do whatever it is the Lord asks of me.

THE VOICE OF THE WILDERNESS

Gideon!

GIDEON

(Looks around, shocked.)
Ah! W-who goes there?

BEING IN WHITE

(Looks up with a smile.)

THE VOICE OF THE WILDERNESS
The Lord God of Abraham, Isaac, and Jacob.

GIDEON
Oh ...
    (Straightens himself up.)
What is it that you require of me?

THE VOICE OF THE WILDERNESS
Tell everyone that you are all on your way to receiving the gifts you desire. But you must seek me more and do my works. For they are not to be read of only, but to be applied as well.

GIDEON
    (Looks at BEING IN WHITE, looks up again.)
You've got it!

BEING IN WHITE
    (Smiles.)
My work here is done. Fear not, for the Lord thy God will be with you through it all.
    (Exits behind door.)

GIDEON
    (Looks at the sleeping men.)
How could you guys still be sleeping after all of that? Men, wake up. Wake up!

ALL (EXCEPT GIDEON)
    (Wake up slowly, but stay on the ground.)
Ugh!

GIDEON
I'm sure by now you know what must have happened. Well, this time it wasn't just the messenger that appeared before me, but the Voice of the

Wilderness. He's telling us to not only fast, pray, and read, but to also apply what we read.

SAMSON

Gideon, normally I'd say we can't argue with that. But how are we supposed to show that we are applying it?

HEZEKIAH

Oh, come on. You really don't know?

SAMSON
(Aggressively walks towards Hezekiah.)
So what if I don't?

JABEZ
(Splits up Hezekiah and Samson.)
Have you forgotten Proverbs 10:14? "Wise men lay up knowledge: but the mouth of the foolish is near destruction."

GIDEON

Along with that, 2 Timothy 2:14–16 says, "Of these things put them in remembrance, charging them before the Lord that they strive not about words to no profit, but to the subverting of the hearers. Study to shew thyself approved unto God, a workman that needeth not to be ashamed, rightly dividing the word of truth. But shun profane and vain babblings: for they will increase unto more ungodliness."

MOSES

Amen! We shall apply the Word along with our fasting, praying, and reading for another seven days, in hopes that we will be granted entrance into the third dimension in the Holy Spirit.

THE VOICE OF THE WILDERNESS
(Sings "Holy Spirit, Thou Art Welcome in This Place.")
(TIME PASSES BY)

GIDEON

(Looks to make sure everyone is asleep, tries to open the door. It is still locked. Goes back to sleep.)

THE VOICE OF THE WILDERNESS

(Stops singing.)

Behold. My men have fasted, prayed, read my Word, and applied it with a seeking heart for my gifts. Yet still the Spirit is willing, but the flesh is weak. I send thou, my messenger, to go before the strongest one among them. Give him a message of foundation and peace.

BEING IN WHITE

I shall.

(Enters stage from behind door.)

Samson.

SAMSON

(Wakes up and stands.)

What? What could we possibly be missing?

(Walks over to BEING IN WHITE.)

BEING IN WHITE

Samson!

SAMSON

I mean, c'mon. We've done practically everything! What more could be asked of us?

BEING IN WHITE

Samson!

SAMSON

What?

BEING IN WHITE

Indeed you have all fasted, prayed, read, and applied the things of God. But I ask you one question …
    (Looks to Samson.)
Do you *love* God?

SAMSON

Do I? Of course I do! Why do you think—

BEING IN WHITE

    (Steps towards Samson, forcing Samson to step back.)
Do you *love* God?

ALL (EXCEPT SAMSON & BEING IN WHITE)

(Wake up and look.)

SAMSON

I made it all this way because I lo—

BEING IN WHITE

    (Looks to everyone.)
Do you love God?

ALL (EXCEPT BEING IN WHITE)

Yes, we do!

BEING IN WHITE

Then I leave you with this. In the twenty-eight days that passed you by, you've done the will of God—that I can't deny. So for the next twelve, I ask that you show love, for the third dimension will take you high up above!
    (Exits behind door.)

ALL (EXCEPT BEING IN WHITE)

(Look at the door.)

SAMSON

"Cause me to hear thy lovingkindness in the morning; for in thee do I trust: cause me to know the way wherein I should walk; for I lift up my soul unto thee." Psalms 143:8. I think I get it now.

MOSES

Amen! We shall show our love for God along with our fasting, praying, reading, and applying for the next twelve days, in hopes that we will be granted entrance into the third dimension in the Holy Spirit.

THE VOICE OF THE WILDERNESS
(Sings "Holy Spirit Come and Fill This Place.")
(TIME PASSES BY)

THE VOICE OF THE WILDERNESS
(Stops singing.)

BEING IN WHITE

Men, wake up! Wake up!

ALL (EXCEPT BEING IN WHITE)
(Wake up and stand.)
We are awake!

THE VOICE OF THE WILDERNESS

Behold. You, my mighty men of valour have fasted, prayed, and read and applied my Word with a seeking heart for my gifts. I ask you now, one question: Do you love me?

ALL (EXCEPT THE VOICE OF THE WILDERNESS)
Hallelujah, we do!

THE VOICE OF THE WILDERNESS

Then it is time to enter the third dimension in the Holy Spirit!

ALL (EXCEPT THE VOICE OF THE WILDERNESS)
(Enters the door, sings "Holy Spirit, Come and Fill This Place," closes door once inside.)
Hallelujah!

THE END

Doors and Strangers

CHARACTERS   ACTORS/ACTRESSES

CHARACTERS	ACTORS/ACTRESSES
Mary (Scatterbrained)	
Delilah (Thrill-seeking)	
Abimelech (Short-tempered)	
Samson (Big Bravado)	
The Stranger (Calm and Sarcastic)	

Guideline

* All character names are centred and in capitals.
* All dialogue is placed under the respective character's name.
* Anything in (brackets) is an action.
* A costume reflecting each respective character is required.

Side Notes

The words next to the names are their personality traits. They'll give you an idea on how to act them out. Highlight your parts! Try to remember the line before yours so you know your cue.

Setting

The front of the sanctuary will be where all scenes take place. There will be a couch in the centre of the stage, a TV remote on a table right next to it, and a backdrop that includes three doors to separate the three rooms. There will be an extra door to the right of the stage angled towards the audience, acting as the apartment entrance. Everyone begins offstage except for Mary.

Scene 1

MARY

(On her knees, praying, with her head on the couch facing away from the audience.)

"And the prayer of faith shall save the sick, and the Lord shall raise him up; and if he have committed sins, they shall be forgiven him."

(Coughs.)

DELILAH

(Enters stage from her room.)

MARY

"Confess your faults one to another, and pray one for another, that ye may be healed. The effectual fervent prayer of a righteous man availeth much." James 5:15–16.

DELILAH

(Sits on the right side of the couch.)

Whatcha doin'?

MARY

(Looks appalled.)

I'm praying. Now, if you don't mind ...

(Puts head back on the couch.)

DELILAH

I won't mind if you won't mind.

(Takes out a cigarette.)

You got a light?

MARY

(Stands up furiously.)

No smoking in the house!

DELILAH

I'll go outside. I was just asking for a light.

MARY

"The Lord is my light and my salvation; whom shall I fear? the Lord is the strength of my life; of whom shall I be afraid?" Psalms 27:1.

DELILAH

(Rolls her eyes.)
Here we go.

MARY

"Let your light so shine before men, that they may see your good works, and glorify your Father which is in heaven." Matthew 5:16.

DELILAH

She's on a role, guys. Someone stop her.

ABIMELECH

(From offstage.)
Not it!

SAMSON

(Enters stage from Delilah's room.)
Aw, man!
(Approaches MARY.)

MARY

"And the light shineth in darkness; and the darkness comprehended it not." John 1:5.

SAMSON

(Forces Mary to sit down in the centre of the couch.)
Mary, don't struggle.

MARY

(Panting.)
I will not suffer …
(Out of breath, looks down.)

SAMSON

(To Delilah.)
Did she take her meds today?

DELILAH

I dunno. I just got up.
(Shows cigarette to Samson.)
You got a light?

SAMSON

Please don't tell me she saw that.

DELILAH

What? I need something to take the edge off. Last night was tiring.
(Winks at Samson.)
Don't act like you didn't have a good time too.

SAMSON

For once, Delilah, I'd like this house to be a place of peace.

DELILAH

You brought her here, Samson. I don't know why you thought rooming with
a psychotic would make this house any more peaceful.

SAMSON

The same reason you thought bringing cigarettes in the house would be
peaceful.

DELILAH

(Stands up, frustrated.)
Ugh! You're always so defensive when it comes to her.

ABIMELECH

(From offstage.)
You two, keep it down! I'm trying to sleep here!

DELILAH

I'll be outside.
(Steps towards the door.)

SAMSON

Why? You don't have a light.

DELILAH

To get away from you, Samson.
(Exits stage through the door.)

SAMSON

(Sighs.)
You okay?
(Sits down beside Mary.)
Silent treatment, huh?

MARY

(Looks carefully at Samson.)
I have a question.

SAMSON

Go ahead.

MARY

Why did you emerge from Delilah's room?

SAMSON

We …

MARY

Before I moved in with you three, you told me this was a house of praise, Samson. You told me you were a man of God and that I could "Rejoice evermore, pray without ceasing," as 1 Thessalonians 5:16–17 says.

SAMSON

Mary, have you taken your medication today?

MARY

(Stands up aggressively.)
Was it all a lie?

SAMSON

I never meant to—

MARY

You just wanted a fourth roommate so you could pay the bills.

SAMSON

(Stands up aggressively.)
That's not ...
(Calms himself down.)
That's not true.

DELILAH

(Enters stage and walks towards her room.)
I'll be in my room, babe.

MARY

(Looks at Delilah, then at Samson.)
First Corinthians 6:18.

DELILAH

Ugh.
(Exits stage into her room.)

MARY

"Flee fornication. Every sin that a man doeth is without the body; but he that committeth fornication sinneth against his own body."

SAMSON

What's fornication?

MARY

(Furiously.)
And you call yourself a man of God? "Marriage is honourable in all, and the bed undefiled: but whoremongers and adulterers God will judge." Hebrews 13:4.

ABIMELECH

(Enters stage, rubbing eyes.)
Does sleep mean nothing to you?

MARY

(Begins to exit stage.)

SAMSON

Wait, where are you going?

MARY

I'm going to cover this house under the blood.
(Exits stage through the door.)

SAMSON

Unbelievable.
(Sits down.)

ABIMELECH

I know—she forgot the knife.
(Sits down.)
Where's she gonna get blood from now?
(Mockingly gestures slitting wrists.)

SAMSON

Not cool, man.

ABIMELECH

I'm kidding. I don't want her dead. I just want her gone.

SAMSON

What? Why? She's harmless.

ABIMELECH

She's psychotic, Samson. Having her around is like having seven devils in the house.

SAMSON

Since when do devils pray?

ABIMELECH

Don't forget, the devil was once an angel.

SAMSON

You know what? I'm done with this!
    (Stands up.)
Delilah.

DELILAH

    (From offstage.)
What?

SAMSON

Get in here!

DELILAH

    (Enters stage with sass.)
Where's the fire, chief?

SAMSON

What's with your vendetta against Mary?

DELILAH

I have a vendetta against her? Anytime I do anything, she gets all mad at
me, telling me I'm some kind of harlot or deceiver. We've never had a normal
conversation. It's always God this and Bible that. I'm cool with her being a
Christian, but she doesn't have to force-feed her beliefs on me.

SAMSON

(Rests his hand on her shoulder.)
She's just looking out for your best interest.

DELILAH

(Slaps his hand off her shoulder and shakes her head.)
Don't.

ABIMELECH

(Laughs.)

SAMSON

You got something to say?

ABIMELECH

Yes. If this is your relationship in three weeks, I can only imagine the
catastrophe in four.

SAMSON

(Grabs Abimelech.)
I'm getting a little tired of your attitude.

ABIMELECH

(Stands up to Samson.)
I'm getting a little tired of your kindness.

SAMSON & ABIMELECH
(Shake each other up.)

DELILAH
Ugh! Don't you see what she's doing us you, guys? Mary's making us fight.

SAMSON
(Still holding Abimelech.)

ABIMELECH
(No longer putting up a fight, sarcastically.
Your girlfriend's right, Samson. We shouldn't fight.

SAMSON
(Pushes Abimelech into his seat.)
Mary doesn't go anywhere, okay? She stays with us, and that's final.
(Exits stage into his room.)

ABIMELECH
(Sarcastically.)
Whatever you say, fearless leader.

DELILAH
(Pulls out cigarette.)
You got a light?

ABIMELECH
Puh! I don't smoke!

DELILAH
(Rolls eyes and exits stage to her room.)

MARY
(Enters stage.)
Oh, Abimelech ... I see you're awake now.

ABIMELECH

No thanks to you, princess. And please, just call me Abi.

MARY

I didn't mean to wake you up, Abimelech.

ABIMELECH

Did you not hear me two seconds ago? Just call me Abi.

MARY

But that isn't your name. Your name is Abimelech.

ABIMELECH

You're a pain, Mary.

MARY

What kind of pain? A pain like Jabez? Or a pain like Jezebel?

ABIMELECH

A pain like Judith.

MARY

I'm not familiar with that character. Did you mean Judas? Or perhaps Jonah? Wait. Where is everyone?

ABIMELECH

They left because of you.

MARY

What?

ABIMELECH

No one wants you here, Mary.

MARY

(Looks off to the side.)
Fine, then. I will leave.

ABIMELECH

(Happily.)
You will?

MARY

You said it yourself. I'm not wanted. I have nothing to fear. "And all these blessings shall come on thee, and overtake thee, if thou shalt hearken unto the voice of the LORD thy God. Blessed shalt thou be in the city, and blessed shalt thou be in the field. Blessed shall be the fruit of thy body, and the fruit of thy ground, and the fruit of thy cattle, the increase of thy kine, and the flocks of thy sheep. Blessed shall be thy basket and thy store. Blessed shalt thou be when thou comest in, and blessed shalt thou be when thou goest out. The LORD shall cause thine enemies that rise up against thee to be smitten before thy face: they shall come out against thee one way, and flee before thee seven ways." Deuteronomy 28:2–7.

ABIMELECH

Uh-huh … So when will you leave?

MARY

Tonight, after I've packed my things. Don't tell anyone, though.

ABIMELECH

My lips are sealed.
    (Exits stage to his room.)

Scene 2

THE STRANGER

(Knocks on the door.)

MARY

(Looks at the door questionably.)

Who is it?

THE STRANGER

"Behold, I stand at the door, and knock: if any man hear my voice, and open the door, I will come in to him, and will sup with him, and he with me."

MARY

Revelation 3:20?

(Rushes to the door.)

Is that Revelation 3:20?

THE STRANGER

Aw, so you remember me?

MARY

I'd never forget. But how can I be sure it's you?

THE STRANGER

"I am the good shepherd, and know my sheep, and am known of mine."

MARY

John 10:14.

(Sigh of relief.)

You may enter.

(Opens the door.)

THE STRANGER

(Enters stage from the door.)

Thank you.

MARY

(Gestures to The Stranger to take a seat)

I have so many questions for you!

THE STRANGER

(Takes a seat.)
And I have answers. But first I must ask, may I have something to eat?

MARY

Oh, um ... we keep all the food in Samson's room. He worries that we'll eat it all when he's not looking. I can get some for you.
(Stands up and rushes to Samson's room.)
Samson! May I have a fish on a plate?

SAMSON

(From offstage.)
What for?

MARY

Come and see for yourself.

SAMSON

I'm a bit busy. Just take it.
(Hands Mary the fish on the plate from offstage.)

MARY

(Rushes back to The Stranger and gives the fish on the plate.)
Here you go. Would you like anything else?

THE STRANGER

I am a little bit thirsty. Maybe—

MARY

Say no more!
(Rushes to Delilah's room.)
Delilah, may I have a bottle of water?

DELILAH

(From offstage.)
So you've finally decided to take your pills, huh?

MARY

I don't need those pills. I have Jesus in my life.

DELILAH

(From offstage.)
I'm not giving you anything unless you take those pills.

MARY

(Marches into Delilah's room.)

DELILAH

(From offstage.)
What are you doing? Get out of my room! Samson, stop her!

SAMSON

I'm a bit busy!

MARY

(Enters stage from Delilah's room with a water bottle.)

DELILAH

(Throws a pillow at Mary.)
You are never coming in here again!

MARY

(Gives The Stranger the water bottle.)

THE STRANGER

You really don't have to—

MARY

You must be cold.
    (Walks over to Abimelech's room.)
Abimelech!

ABIMELECH

No!

MARY

I just want a blanket.

ABIMELECH

(Enters stage from his room with the blanket.)

Fine, here.

(Shocked to see The Stranger, pushes Mary out of the way.)

Excuse me, sir! You must be lost.

(Walks over to The Stranger aggressively.)

You see, this is our house, not a shelter for the homeless.

MARY

How dare you!

THE STRANGER

(Stands up.)

"Judge not, that ye be not judged. For with what judgment ye judge, ye shall be judged: and with what measure ye mete, it shall be measured to you again." Matthew 7:1–2.

ABIMELECH

Look here. This house is problematic enough with one Christian. The last thing we need here is another.

THE STRANGER

Then I will be on my way.

(Walks towards the door.)

MARY

(Rushes to stop The Stranger.)

But—

THE STRANGER

"Be strong and of a good courage, fear not, nor be afraid of them: for the LORD thy God, he it is that doth go with thee; he will not fail thee, nor forsake thee." Deuteronomy 31:6.

MARY

But I don't want you to—

THE STRANGER

"Behold, I send you forth as sheep in the midst of wolves: be ye therefore wise as serpents, and harmless as doves." Matthew 10:16.

MARY

(Cries.)
Please don't go!
(Falls to her knees and touches the hem of his garment, is in a state of shock.)

THE STRANGER

(Exits stage through the door.)

DELILAH

(Enters stage simultaneously.)
What's with all the noise?

ABIMELECH

(Sits down.)
Mary's having another one of her episodes.

MARY

W-what? You saw him too! Don't act like you didn't see him.

ABIMELECH

There's no one in the room but us three.

MARY

There was a fourth man!

DELILAH

You mean Samson? Ugh. Mary, you need to take your pills!

MARY

I am not crazy!

SAMSON

(Enters stage.)
Enough!

DELILAH

(Sits next to Abimelech.)
Mary, take a seat.

MARY

No! "Blessed *is* the man that walketh not in the counsel of the ungodly, nor standeth in the way of sinners, nor sitteth in the seat of the scornful." Psalm 1:1.

SAMSON

Then sit where you want to, Mary.
(Looks to Abimelech and Delilah.)
What happened?

DELILAH

Mary said she saw someone in the house.

SAMSON

Did she?

ABIMELECH

No, she was probably hallucinating.

SAMSON

Mary. Did you?

MARY

Yes. I saw a stranger at the door. I believe it was—

DELILAH

And your first instinct was to let them in? Samson, don't you see what's
wrong here?

ABIMELECH

Yeah, Samson!

SAMSON

Settle down, guys.

DELILAH

(Stands up.)
No, I will *not* settle down. Why do you keep her around?

SAMSON

That's private.

DELILAH

How can you say you love me when you won't confide in me?

ABIMELECH

Isn't it obvious, Delilah? He loves her more than you.

SAMSON

Quiet, you!

DELILAH

Is that true, Samson? Does what we have mean nothing to you?

SAMSON

You want to know why? You all what to know why? It's because I fear the Lord!

ABIMELECH & DELILAH

What?

MARY

"The fear of the Lord is the instruction of wisdom; and before honour is humility." Proverbs 15:33.

DELILAH

(To Mary.)
Excuse me? You don't get to talk.

ABIMELECH

So you're a Christian too? I guess you're more of a casual Christian, then.

SAMSON

Call it whatever you want. Before we moved in together, I remember you both telling me that you'd respect the house rules. Three of which were not to curse, not to smoke, and not to cheat the house bill. But within a month, you broke those. So I figured we could use a balance. I'd let another Christian room with us, and she'd bless the house.

MARY

Wait. Is that all I am to you? Just someone who can pray over our food and our finances and our house?

SAMSON

No … no.

MARY

(Stands up and walks over to Samson.)
What about my health, Samson? What about my well-being?

SAMSON

I ...

(Looks to Delilah and Abimelech.)
A little help here?

ABIMELECH & DELILAH

(Both take a seat.)

ABIMELECH

(Sarcastically.)
You're doing a great job by yourself.

DELILAH

(Sarcastically.)
Yes, don't let us get in the way.

SAMSON

Look, Mary, I didn't think—

MARY

You're right. You didn't think. I'm leaving tonight.

SAMSON & DELILAH

What?

MARY

I've had enough of you all. Now, get out of my room.

ABIMELECH

Technically, this is the living room.

MARY

(Gives Abimelech a death glare.)

ABIMELECH

I'll be in my room.
(Exits stage into his room.)

DELILAH

(Walks over to Samson.)
Don't let her intimidate you.
(Exits stage to her room.)

SAMSON

(Touches Mary's shoulder.)

MARY

(Shakes her head and backs away.)

SAMSON

(Exits to his room.)

Scene 3

MARY

(Takes a seat and writes something down on a piece of paper.)
Now I just have to pack.
(Puts the paper on the table next to her, pulls a bag from behind the couch, and begins packing some things.)

THE STRANGER

(Knocks at the door.)

MARY

(Puts packed bag behind the couch and opens the door excitedly.)
I knew you'd be back.

THE STRANGER

(Enters stage from the door carrying a blanket and a bag.)
Actually, I came back to return your blanket.

MARY

(Takes blanket disappointedly.)

That's all?

THE STRANGER

Well, no, actually. There are a few questions of yours to which I have the answers. I am ready when you are.

MARY

(Gestures for both of them to take a seat.)

Why am I sick? I pray every day and read the Bible, but I still need to take those pills.

THE STRANGER

(Takes a seat.)

To make a long answer short, it's okay to see a doctor. Just be sure to pray before you do. Pray that God will give you the right doctor for the right occasion, and pray against pills that can warp the mind or disfigure your face. Do you remember Matthew 9:12? Or even Mark 2:17?

MARY

Yes, I know those scriptures. Are you implying that I'm all right?

THE STRANGER

Do you remember our previous encounter? Before I left—

MARY

-Before you left, I touched the hem of your garment. I instantly felt better.

THE STRANGER

So you need not question your sickness.

MARY

Is Samson truly a man of God?

THE STRANGER

Samson must make his own decision: to tarry with the seductress or to enter my kingdom free of lust. Either way, we should not force him. You have advised him time and time again, and he hasn't heeded your word. But I believe he too can have a change of heart. But never forget, "Not everyone who says to me, 'Lord, Lord,' will enter the kingdom of heaven, but only the one who does the will of my Father who is in heaven. Many will say to me on that day, 'Lord, Lord, did we not prophesy in your name and in your name drive out demons and in your name perform many miracles?' Then I will tell them plainly, 'I never knew you. Away from me, you evildoers!'" Matthew 7:21–23.

MARY

What about the others? Are they too far gone to save?

THE STRANGER

For the others, keep them in prayer. The enemy will use people closest to you, both figuratively and literally, to turn against you. So pray against the plans of the enemy. Ephesians 6:12 says, "For we wrestle not against flesh and blood, but against principalities, against powers, against the rulers of the darkness of this world, against spiritual wickedness in high places."

MARY

Then ... Should I really go?

THE STRANGER

It would seem you've already made up your mind about leaving.

MARY

It's not that I don't want to help. It's just that I don't feel accepted here.

THE STRANGER

"And he said, Verily I say unto you, No prophet is accepted in his own country." Luke 4:24.

MARY

I don't understand. Are you telling me to stay or to go?

THE STRANGER

You have to make that choice on your own. Excuse me.
   (Walks by Mary.)
Samson, Delilah, Abimelech.

MARY

   (In shock.)
How do you know their names?

THE STRANGER

You did say them earlier.

SAMSON, DELILAH & ABIMELECH

   (Enter stage from their respective rooms.)

SAMSON

   (To Mary.)
Who is this, Mary? Is this the stranger you saw earlier?

ABIMELECH

I've never seen him before.

DELILAH

Me neither.

THE STRANGER

   (Stands in the middle.)
Don't act like I'm not here. Come and stand by my side. All of you.

ABIMELECH

   (To Samson.)
If he makes any sudden movements, we jump him.

SAMSON

Got it.

SAMSON & MARY

(Stand on his right side.)

DELILAH & ABIMELECH

(Stand on his left side.)

THE STRANGER

Ha! Know ye not of Matthew 25:33–46? Mary, reach into my bag and fetch me my five Bibles. Give one to each of them.

MARY

(Gets the Bibles from his bag.)

DELILAH

Oh, no! Samson, do something about this. I'm not being forced to—

SAMSON

The quicker we read it, the quicker he gets out of here, Delilah.

THE STRANGER

I will never leave you.

ABIMELECH

Great, another loon.

MARY

(Gives everyone a Bible.)
"And he shall set the sheep on his right hand, but the goats on the left. Then shall the King say unto them on his right hand, Come, ye blessed of my Father, inherit the kingdom prepared for you from the foundation of the world: For I was an hungred, and ye gave me meat: I was thirsty, and ye gave me drink: I was a stranger, and ye took me in:" Matthew 25:33–35.

THE STRANGER

Samson, continue.

SAMSON

"Naked, and ye clothed me: I was sick, and ye visited me: I was in prison, and ye came unto me. Then shall the righteous answer him, saying, Lord, when saw we thee an hungred, and fed thee? or thirsty, and gave thee drink? When saw we thee a stranger, and took thee in? or naked, and clothed thee? Or when saw we thee sick, or in prison, and came unto thee?" Matthew 25:36–39.

THE STRANGER

"And the King shall answer and say unto them, Verily I say unto you, Inasmuch as ye have done it unto one of the least of these my brethren, ye have done it unto me." Matthew 25:40. Delilah, you may continue.

DELILAH

(Sigh.)
"Then shall he say also unto them on the left hand, Depart from me, ye cursed, into everlasting fire, prepared for the devil and his angels: For I was an hungred, and ye gave me no meat: I was thirsty, and ye gave me no drink: I was a stranger, and ye took me not in: naked, and ye clothed me not: sick, and in prison, and ye visited me not." Matthew 25:41–43.

THE STRANGER

Abimelech.

ABIMELECH

"Then shall they also answer him, saying, Lord, when saw we thee an hungred, or athirst, or a stranger, or naked, or sick, or in prison, and did not minister unto thee? Then shall he answer them, saying, Verily I say unto you, Inasmuch as ye did it not to one of the least of these, ye did it not to me. And these shall go away into everlasting punishment: but the righteous into life eternal." Matthew 25:44–46.

MARY

Do you guys understand now?

DELILAH

(Gives the Bible back to The Stranger.)
Uh, no!

MARY

Wow, really?

ABIMELECH

(Gives the Bible back to The Stranger.)
I don't get it either. We did what you wanted, stranger. Now please won't you kindly get out of our house?

THE STRANGER

(Walks to the door, picking up the Bibles and putting them in his bag as he leaves.)

MARY

If he leaves, I'm going with him.

THE STRANGER

Are you sure, Mary?

MARY

(Takes her packed bag from behind the couch and walks towards the door.)
I've never been so sure of anything in my life.

ABIMELECH

(To Samson.)
He's taking your girl, Samson.

DELILAH

Ugh!
(To Abimelech.)
His girl is standing right here!

MARY

Samson, come with us.
(Reaches her hand out.)
You don't have to question yourself anymore. All the answers are here.

SAMSON

(Walks towards the door.)

DELILAH

If you love me, Samson, you'll stay.

SAMSON

(Stops moving in the middle of the stage and turns towards Delilah and Abimelech.)

DELILAH

Think of all the fun we can have once she's gone.

ABIMELECH

No more judgmental Mary.

MARY

(Still reaching.)
Samson, don't.

DELILAH

(Sarcastically.)
Yes, Samson, don't have fun, don't enjoy life, don't trust your friends.

THE STRANGER

Samson.

SAMSON

(Turns towards The Stranger.)

THE STRANGER

"Thus saith the LORD; Cursed *be* the man that trusteth in man, and maketh flesh his arm, and whose heart departeth from the LORD." Jeremiah 17:5.

ABIMELECH

Samson, we need a man to pay the bills.

SAMSON

(Walks towards Abimelech and Delilah.)
I'm sorry, Mary.

DELILAH

(Holds Samson's shoulders and sticks her tongue out at Mary.)

THE STRANGER & MARY

(Exit stage through the door.)

ABIMELECH & DELILAH

(High-five)
Yes!
(Exit stage excitedly to their respective rooms.)

SAMSON

(Sits down saddened, sees the piece of paper Mary left behind, picks it up, and reads it)

MARY

Dear Samson, in case you ever want to visit, here's my new address: 7367 Magdalene Avenue. At least that's where I hope I'll be able to move in. While I'm away, I hope you'll keep this close to your heart. "Therefore also now, saith the LORD, turn ye even to me with all your heart, and with fasting, and with weeping, and with mourning: And rend your heart, and not your garments, and turn unto the LORD your God: for he is gracious and merciful, slow to anger, and of great kindness, and repenteth him of the evil." Joel 2:12–13.

SAMSON
(Looks back to see if the other two are gone, stands up, looks at the audience, and exits stage through the door.)

THE END

Lights, Camera, Spiritual Fruits

CHARACTERS	ACTORS/ACTRESSES
Judge 1	
Judge 2	
Judge 3	
Candidate 1/Rachel (Fear, Love)	
Candidate 2/Hannah (Sorrow, Joy)	
Candidate 3/ Abigail (Distress, Peace)	
Candidate 4/Peter (Impatience, Longsuffering)	
Candidate 5/Joshua (Harshness, Gentleness)	
Candidate 6/Saul/Paul (Wickedness, Goodness)	
Candidate 7/Caleb (Doubt, Faith)	
Candidate 8/Jonah (Immodest, Meekness)	
Candidate 9/David (Wild, Temperance)	

Guideline

* All character names are centred and in capitals.
* All dialogue is placed under the respective character's name.
* Anything in (brackets) is an action.
* A costume reflecting each respective character is required.

Side Notes

The words next to the names are personality traits. They'll give you an idea on how to act them out. Highlight your parts! And try to remember the line before yours so you know your cue.

Setting

The front of the sanctuary will be where all scenes take place. There will be three seats to the left of the stage tilted diagonally towards the audience. The nine candidates start on stage, each rehearsing their lines in a different way. The judges start offstage.

ALL (EXCEPT JUDGES 1, 2 & 3)
(Stand completely still, in silence.)

RACHEL
(Pacing back and forth.)

SAUL
(Trips Rachel.)

RACHEL
(Bumps into Joshua.)

JOSHUA
(Lifts her off of him and pushes her away.)
What's wrong with you? You got two left feet?

RACHEL
(Bumps into David.)

DAVID
(Turns around excitedly.)
Hey! I can tell you're pumped for the audition.
(Starts stretching.)
I think you've got the right idea. A little cardio before the performance of a life time should do me some good.
(Accidentally pushes Rachel while stretching.)

RACHEL
(Bumps into Jonah.)
S-sorry.

JONAH
(Looks away in disgust.)
Lord, why are you doing this to me? What have I done to deserve this? I have lost my focus because of this girl.

RACHEL

I said I was sorry.

HANNAH

(Weeping.)

RACHEL

(Walks over to Hannah.)
What's wrong?

HANNAH

No one loves me!

RACHEL

(Backs up startled, accidentally bumps into Abigail, and falls onto the floor.)

ABIGAIL

(Sighs.)
Please go away. I'm trying to practice here …

CALEB

Should I help? I don't know … Maybe yes, maybe no.

PETER

(Grabs Rachel by the shoulder and gets her back on her feet.)
Would you hurry it up? The amateurs are getting rowdy!

RACHEL

I'm not.

JUDGES 1, 2 & 3

(Enter stage and take a seat.)

PETER

Well?

JUDGE 3

Yes?

PETER

Sorry you're late?

JUDGE 2

We're not late. You're all just early.

SAUL

Great. So can we get started?

JUDGE 2

Yes, but first we'd like to say thank you all for coming to audition for the next instalment of *Let There Be Laughs*.

JUDGE 1

As you know, we'll be looking for your ability to wow the crowed. We know you can all take constructive criticism and pointers from the judges.

JUDGE 3

Don't you know?

JUDGES 1, 2 & 3

I will never give you more than you can handle.

JUDGE 3

So, who's first?

SAUL

(Pushes Rachel forward.)

RACHEL

N-no, I don't—

JUDGE 1

Excellent! It has been decided!

JUDGE 2

You'll do fine, don't you worry.

JUDGE 3

Are you ready?

RACHEL

I guess so.

ALL (EXCEPT JUDGES 1, 2, 3 & RACHEL)
(Exit stage.)

JUDGE 3

Which part are you auditioning for?

RACHEL

I'm auditioning for the part of Rachel. I'll be using parts of Genesis 30 for reference.

JUDGE 2

You may begin whenever you're ready.

RACHEL

(Say nervously.)
"Behold my maid Bilhah, go in unto her; and she shall bear upon my knees, that I may also have children by her." Genesis 30:3. "God hath judged me, and hath also heard my voice, and hath given me a son." Genesis 30:6. "With great wrestling's have I wrestled with my sister, and I have prevailed." Genesis 30:8. How was that?

JUDGE 3

You seem very afraid. Is there something on your mind?

JUDGE 1

She obviously has no faith in this project.

JUDGE 2

She just needs more confidence, is all.

JUDGE 3

Confidence isn't the opposite of fear. You know what is?

JUDGE 1

Yes, of course. It's love.

RACHEL

Love?

JUDGE 2

Yes, you need to put more love into it. It'll get rid of any stage fright you're experiencing.

RACHEL

So what now?

JUDGE 1

Just wait outside. We'll call you in when we're ready for you again. Send in candidates four and six, please.

RACHEL

(Exits stage.)

PETER & SAUL

(Enter stage,)

JUDGE 3

Which parts are you auditioning for?

PETER

I'm auditioning for the part of Peter. I'll be using Acts 2:38 for reference.

SAUL

And I'll be auditioning for the part of Paul. I'll be using Galatians 2:14 for reference.

JUDGE 2

You may begin whenever you're ready.

PETER

(Say over-confidently)
"Lord, if it be thou, bid me come unto thee on the water."

SAUL

(Say with snark.)
"If thou, being a Jew, livest after the manner of Gentiles, and not as do the Jews, why compellest thou the Gentiles to live as do the Jews?"

JUDGE 1

Is that all?

SAUL

No! My line should be first here!
(Pushes Peter.)

PETER

I couldn't wait for your slow delivery. I need them to see me now!

JUDGE 2

But you said you were reading Acts 2:38.

SAUL

(Snickers.)

PETER

Wasn't I?

JUDGE 1

That was Matthew 14:28, what you just said.

PETER

(Turns to Saul.)
You told me that that was the right scripture!

SAUL

Only because I knew you'd be too impatient to check it over.

PETER

How could you be so wicked?

JUDGE 3

Both of you! Why are you fighting?

JUDGE 2

Candidate four, you shouldn't be so hasty. Always read over the Word before you bring it here.

JUDGE 1

Candidate six, you must not be so wicked! Especially to your teammate. Sabotaging the work of fellows is never right. You've got a long journey to travel.

JUDGE 3

Damascus is still a distance away, but you'll make it. Candidate four, impatience can only be combated with longsuffering. Candidate six, wickedness must not try to overthrow goodness. Beat the wickedness with goodness. Why not give it a try?

SAUL

Whatever. I'm outta here.
    (Exits stage.)

PETER

This isn't the last you've seen of me, either.
    (Exits stage)

JUDGE 1

Candidates five and seven, you may enter.

JOSHUA

    (Enters stage.)
You called?

CALEB

    (Enters stage.)
I'm pretty sure they called. Well, to be more specific, they shouted. Or perhaps the better term would be they exclaimed? No, wait ... I guess *called* works best. What do you think?

JUDGE 1

What on earth are you wearing?

JOSHUA

Tuxedos. You see, our characters are spies, so I figured we'd try to grasp the character by dressing the part, you know?

JUDGE 1

A good actor wouldn't need to rely on costumes alone.

CALEB

Oh, don't worry.
    (Pulls out script)
We brought our scripts too.

JUDGE 3

You guys didn't come prepared?

CALEB

(Holds up finger and reads script carefully.)
No ... we ... didn't. Ha, nailed it.

JOSHUA

(Sighs)
What does the line say underneath this one?

CALEB

(Reads the script.)
Caleb ... don't read the script. Oh ...

JUDGE 3

Um, which part are you auditioning for?

JOSHUA

I'm auditioning for the part of Joshua. I'll be using Numbers 14:7–9 for reference.

CALEB

I'm auditioning for the part of Caleb. I'll be using Numbers 14:7–9 as well.

JUDGE 2

You may begin whenever you're ready.

JOSHUA

(Say aggressively and melodramatically.)
"The land, which we passed through to search it, is an exceeding good land."
Numbers 14:7.

CALEB

(Say with gaps in between parts and look back at the script each time.)
"If the Lord delight in us, then he will bring us into this land, and give it
us; a land which floweth with milk and honey." Numbers 14:8.

JOSHUA

(Say aggressively and melodramatically.)
"Only rebel not ye against the Lord, neither fear ye the people of the land;
for they are bread for us: their defence is departed from them, and the Lord
is with us: fear them not." Numbers 14:9.

JUDGE 1

This one should be pretty obvious. Candidate five, you are too harsh; try a
little gentleness. Candidate seven, you are doubtful; you need more faith.
Faith will allow you to do things you could never imagine.

JOSHUA & CALEB

(Exit stage.)

JUDGE 3

What? You're just going to walk away?

JUDGE 2

Let them go. If they really want it, they'll take those words into account.

JUDGE 1

Hmm. You didn't say much that time.

JUDGE 2

It wasn't in the script.
  (Smiles.)

JUDGE 1

(Shakes head.)
Candidates two and three, come in.

HANNAH

(Enters stage with her head down.)

ABIGAIL

(Enters stage.)
Not this again.

JUDGE 3

What's wrong?

ABIGAIL

I don't even care at this point. Let's get this over with.

JUDGE 3

Which part are you auditioning for?

HANNAH

(Looks up, says nothing, and looks back down.)

ABIGAIL

(Sigh.)
She's auditioning for the part of Hannah, using 1 Samuel 1:11 for reference.
I am auditioning for the part of Abigail, using 1 Samuel 25:19 for reference.

JUDGE 2

You may begin whenever you're ready.

HANNAH

(Say while weeping.)
"O LORD of hosts, if thou wilt indeed look on the affliction of thine handmaid, and remember me, and not forget thine handmaid, but wilt give unto thine handmaid a man child, then I will give him unto the LORD all the days of his life, and there shall no razor come upon his head."

ABIGAIL

(Say with distress.)
"Go on before me; behold, I come after you."

JUDGE 2

Candidate three, you seem distressed.

ABIGAIL

No, no … Just getting into character.

JUDGE 3

Abigail?

ABIGAIL

My interpretation, at least.

JUDGE 1

Why would a character so smart be interpreted as someone so distressed?

ABIGAIL

(With sass.)
Have you read about Solomon?

JUDGE 2

Whoa, cool off. This is no time for sass. You seem to be experiencing a high amount of distress. You need to find peace. As for you, candidate two, trade in your sorrow for joy.

HANNAH

(Sniffles.)
Okay.
(Exits stage.)

ABIGAIL

Peace isn't exactly something you can find.
(Exits stage.)

JUDGE 1

Candidates eight and nine, get in here.

JONAH

(Enters stage, looking around.)

DAVID

(Enters stage, jogging.)

JUDGE 3

Is everything okay, candidate nine?

DAVID

Yup, yes, yeah, you got it.

JUDGE 3

Which part are you auditioning for?

JONAH

I'm auditioning for the part of Jonah. I will be using Jonah 4:3, 9 for reference.

DAVID

I'm auditioning for the part of David. I will be using 1 Samuel 17:45–46 for reference.

JUDGE 2

You may begin whenever you're ready.

JONAH

(Say bitterly.)
"It is better for me to die than to live.... I do well to be angry, even unto death."

DAVID

(Say while moving around.)

"Thou comest to me with a sword, and with a spear, and with a shield: but I come to thee in the name of the Lord of hosts, the God of the armies of Israel, whom thou hast defied. This day will the Lord deliver thee into mine hand; and I will smite thee, and take thine head from thee; and I will give the carcases of the host of the Philistines this day unto the fowls of the air, and to the wild beasts of the earth; that all the earth may know that there is a God in Israel."

JUDGE 2

Your delivery seems a bit immodest. Perhaps you need a little more meekness, candidate eight.

JUDGE 1

Good choice for scripture, candidate nine. You just need to be a bit less wild. Learn self-control—temperance, if you will.

JUDGE 3

Wait a minute! I have an idea! All candidates, please enter.

CANDADIATES 1, 2, 3, 4, 5, 6 & 7

(Enter stage.)

JUDGE 3

(Takes the script from candidate seven, writes on it.)

Here is the new script, everyone. Pass it around and read it.

RACHEL

(Takes script.)

Galatians 5:22–23. "But the fruit of the Spirit is love." First John 4:18 says, "There is no fear in love; but perfect love casteth out fear: because fear hath torment. He that feareth is not made perfect in love."

(Passes script.)

HANNAH

(Takes script.)

Galatians 5:22–23. "But the fruit of the Spirit is love, joy." Psalm 30:5 says, "For his anger *endureth but* a moment; in his favour *is* life: weeping may endure for a night, but joy *cometh* in the morning."

(Passes script.)

ABIGAIL

(Takes script.)

Galatians 5:22–23. "But the fruit of the Spirit is love, joy, peace." Philippians 4:7 says, "And the peace of God, which passeth all understanding, shall keep your hearts and minds through Christ Jesus."

(Passes script.)

PETER

(Takes script.)

Galatians 5:22–23. "But the fruit of the Spirit is love, joy, peace, longsuffering." Second Peter 3:9 says, "The Lord is not slack concerning his promise, as some men count slackness; but is longsuffering to us-ward, not willing that any should perish, but that all should come to repentance."

(Passes script.)

JOSHUA

(Takes script.)

Galatians 5:22–23. "But the fruit of the Spirit is love, joy, peace, longsuffering, gentleness." Titus 3:2 says, "To speak evil of no man, to be no brawlers, but gentle, shewing all meekness unto all men."

(Passes script.)

SAUL

(Takes script.)

Galatians 5:22–23. "But the fruit of the Spirit is love, joy, peace, longsuffering, gentleness, goodness …"

PAUL

Galatians 6:10 says, "As we have therefore opportunity, let us do good unto all men, especially unto them who are of the household of faith."

(Passes script.)

CALEB

(Takes script.)

Galatians 5:22–23. "But the fruit of the Spirit is love, joy, peace, longsuffering, gentleness, goodness, faith." Matthew 17:20 says, "And Jesus said unto them, Because of your unbelief: for verily I say unto you, If ye have faith as a grain of mustard seed, ye shall say unto this mountain, Remove hence to yonder place; and it shall remove; and nothing shall be impossible unto you."

(Passes script.)

JONAH

(Takes script.)

Galatians 5:22–23. "But the fruit of the Spirit is love, joy, peace, longsuffering, gentleness, goodness, faith, meekness." Matthew 5:5 says, "Blessed *are* the meek: for they shall inherit the earth."

(Passes script.)

DAVID

(Takes script.)

Galatians 5:22–23. "But the fruit of the Spirit is love, joy, peace, longsuffering, gentleness, goodness, faith, meekness, temperance." Proverbs 29:11 says, "A fool uttereth all his mind: but a wise man keepeth it in till afterwards."

JUDGES 1, 2 & 3

(Walk centre stage.)

Galatians 5:22–23. "But the fruit of the Spirit is love, joy, peace, longsuffering, gentleness, goodness, faith, meekness, temperance: against such there is no law."

THE END

I Know My Bible

CHARACTERS	ACTORS/ACTRESSES
Blue (Nonchalant, Passive-Aggressive, Vain)	
Orange (Gregarious, Intolerant, Forthright)	

Guideline

* All character names are centred and in capitals.
* All dialogue is placed under the respective character's name.
* Anything in (brackets) is an action.
* Not many actions will be given, so be creative.
* A costume reflecting each respective character is required.

Setting

The front of the sanctuary will be where all scenes take place. Both characters are offstage at the beginning of the play. Centre stage, there is a table with a case of dominos behind it and two chairs, one on the left and one on the right.

BLUE & ORANGE
(Enter stage simultaneously. One sits on the left chair, and the other sits on the right chair.)

BLUE
(Sits down.)
It's been a while.

ORANGE
(Sits down.)
Well, whose fault is that?

BLUE
Yes, yes, you're right. I take full responsibility.

ORANGE
Aha, so time has changed you.

BLUE
No, God has changed me.

ORANGE
And your faith hasn't changed at all.

BLUE
It's never been a problem before.

ORANGE
Because you've never had to fight for your faith. You've always struck me as someone who is only faithful because it's convenient.

BLUE
Please do tell about how much greater your faith is than mine. I came all this way just to be ridiculed for the way I believe. Go on—tell me how much better you are.

ORANGE

If you insist.

(Stands up.)

To me, faith is much more than believing; it's living. Have you tried to put yourself in the shoes of some of the people who died for their beliefs?

BLUE

No.

ORANGE

Why not? I expect better from you. Roman 14:8 says, "For whether we live, we live unto the Lord; and whether we die, we die unto the Lord: whether we live therefore, or die, we are the Lord's."

BLUE

I think you're twisting the meaning for your own convenience.

ORANGE

Then I can give you another scripture. Philippians 1:21 says, "For to me to live *is* Christ, and to die *is* gain."

BLUE

Ah. But you're forgetting Psalm 118:17, which says, "I shall not die, but live, and declare the works of the LORD."

ORANGE

(Sits down.)

But that doesn't mean you'll never die.

BLUE

Well, yes and no. Yes, because the flesh will die. No, because God will grant me eternal life.

ORANGE

Hmph.

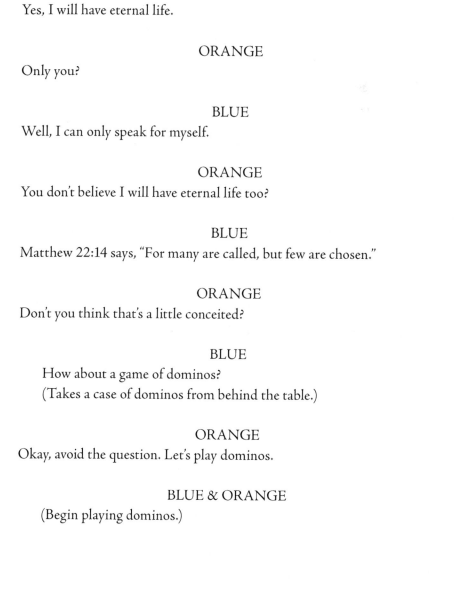

BLUE

What?

ORANGE

Grant you eternal life?

BLUE

Yes, I will have eternal life.

ORANGE

Only you?

BLUE

Well, I can only speak for myself.

ORANGE

You don't believe I will have eternal life too?

BLUE

Matthew 22:14 says, "For many are called, but few are chosen."

ORANGE

Don't you think that's a little conceited?

BLUE

How about a game of dominos?
(Takes a case of dominos from behind the table.)

ORANGE

Okay, avoid the question. Let's play dominos.

BLUE & ORANGE

(Begin playing dominos.)

ORANGE

Proverbs 11:2 says, "When pride cometh, then cometh shame: but with the lowly is wisdom."

BLUE

Is that what you are? Wise because of your boldness? I don't think you know this but there's a thin line between valour and recklessness.

ORANGE

I'm reckless because I know God will protect me.

BLUE

So you admit to being reckless?

ORANGE

Daniel was protected in the lion's den.

BLUE

Daniel didn't go into the lion's den because he wanted to. Daniel went into the lion's den because he was forced to. God protected him from the plans of his enemies.

ORANGE

Okay, okay. I'm only reckless when I know it's right.

BLUE

Think.

ORANGE

What?

BLUE

Think. You're only reckless when you *think* it's right, not when you know.

ORANGE

What are you talking about?

BLUE

If a man spends his life doing what he thinks is right, and he never gets reprimanded for it, are his actions right?

ORANGE

What kind of pretentious drivel are you trying to feed me?

BLUE

Did you just follow the word *pretentious* with *drivel?*

ORANGE

Mockingly.

BLUE

Thanks for that justification.

ORANGE

No problem. To answer your question: yes, he is right.

BLUE

He is right, or you think he's right?

ORANGE

What's the difference?

BLUE

You're really not getting it, are you?

ORANGE

Are you ever going to lose that "I'm better than you" attitude?

BLUE

Are you ever going to lose that "All or nothing" attitude?

BLUE & ORANGE

(Stare at each other in silence.)

ORANGE

Let's talk about something else.

BLUE

Like?

ORANGE

Slavery.

BLUE

(Sarcastically.)
Yay, I thought we'd never get to that topic.

ORANGE

No, seriously. Let's talk about it. Isn't it weird how the Bible gives instruction on slavery?

BLUE

It does?

ORANGE

Someone needs to spend more time in the Old Testament. Deuteronomy 15:12–15 says, "And if thy brother, an Hebrew man, or an Hebrew woman, be sold unto thee, and serve thee six years; then in the seventh year thou shalt let him go free from thee. And when thou sendest him out free from thee, thou shalt not let him go away empty: Thou shalt furnish him liberally out of thy flock, and out of thy floor, and out of thy winepress: of that wherewith the Lord thy God hath blessed thee thou shalt give unto him. And thou shalt remember that thou wast a bondman in the land of Egypt, and the Lord thy God redeemed thee: therefore I command thee this thing to day."

BLUE

What about it?

ORANGE

I think it's weird, because it says to treat slaves nicely. But why would they have slaves in the first place?

BLUE

Because slavery didn't exactly mean the same thing it does today.

ORANGE

Really? Do tell.

BLUE

It was a matter of social status and how much money someone had. In order to make more money, some people decided to be servants for a set amount of years. It wasn't all about race and prejudice. These rules were written so people would know to treat their servants nicely. Because let's face it: people go crazy with power. God saw this and made sure we wouldn't step out of line.

ORANGE

About time you used that brain of yours to some good use. Do you have any sources for that information?

BLUE

Nope. You're just going to have to take my word for it.

ORANGE

Thank goodness this isn't a school paper, huh?

BLUE

Indeed.

ORANGE

I was going to ask about Exodus. Was that an exception to God's rule? But then I remembered Psalm 34:19, which says, "Many *are* the afflictions of the righteous: but the LORD delivereth him out of them all."

BLUE

I think Psalm 37:25 is more fitting. "I have been young, and *now* am old; yet have I not seen the righteous forsaken, nor his seed begging bread."

ORANGE

It's not a competition, you know.

BLUE

You're right. A competition implies I stand a chance of losing.

ORANGE

What was that?

BLUE

Nothing important.

BLUE & ORANGE

(Play dominos in silence.)

ORANGE

You ever feel like everything you say goes over people's head? Like, they only hear the first half of what you're saying and then doze off somewhere in the middle?

BLUE

You don't know the half of it.

ORANGE

I feel like people have lost their ability to listen. Or maybe comprehend would be a better way to put it.

BLUE

You're making some hasty generalizations there, don't you think?

ORANGE

Really think about it.

BLUE

Did you even hear what I said?

ORANGE

Huh? No, look. What I'm saying is, our lack of listening skills extends not only to ourselves, but also to God.

BLUE

All hypocrisy aside, I think I get what you mean. How can people expect to hear from God if they can't even listen to another human being?

ORANGE

Yeah. It's sort of like 1 John 4:20, which says, "If a man say, I love God, and hateth his brother, he is a liar: for he that loveth not his brother whom he hath seen, how can he love God whom he hath not seen?"

BLUE

That's ... surprisingly accurate. Good job.

ORANGE

Don't talk down to me.

BLUE

I'm talking in front of you.

ORANGE

Keep talking like that, and see what happens.

BLUE

Silly me. Here I thought we could have a civil conversation. But instead, you threaten me like a savage.

ORANGE

It's not a threat.

BLUE

It's a promise?

ORANGE

No. What goes around comes around.

BLUE

You got a scripture for that?

ORANGE

Isaiah 3:11 says, "Woe unto the wicked! *it shall be* ill *with him*: for the reward of his hands shall be given him."

BLUE

The wicked huh? Matthew 7:1–2, says, "Judge not, that ye be not judged. For with what judgment ye judge, ye shall be judged: and with what measure ye mete, it shall be measured to you again."

ORANGE

Galatians 6:7, says, "Do not be deceived: God is not mocked, for whatever one sows, that will he also reap."

BLUE

(Checks watch.)
Would you look at the time? Seems our biblical conversation of epic proportion will have to continue next time.
(Stands up and reaches to shake hand.)
You brought up some good scriptures today.

ORANGE

(Stands up and shakes hand.)
I guess you could say I know my Bible.

THE END

About the Author

Ever since I was 8 years old, I enjoyed telling stories. I'd make funny stories, I'd make sad stories, but I was always told that I was an excellent story teller. Little did I know, this would hold true for the rest of my life. As an aspiring Pastor, I make it my mission to follow the will of God and not my own, showing my love by praying, fasting, reading his word regularly, and of course by honouring my father and my mother. They were the first people to ever listen to my stories and would always give me an honest critique afterwards. For as long as I can remember, they always encouraged me to follow my dreams and aim to become what I wanted to be. The problem was, I didn't know exactly what I wanted to be in life. It was through high school, while taking drama classes that I realized what I really wanted to become. You see, I was writing scripts without abandon. The inspiration would hit me and I'd take off, and jot down the ideas. After school was over, I'd start to test some ideas for character interactions and settings. I just loved writing scripts. Some may have even said I was going crazy. To them I'd say "True love doesn't make you crazy, it keeps you sane." A lot of years and even more love was put into it, so I hope you love reading it, as much as I loved writing it.

Printed in the United States
By Bookmasters